IDEAWISE

IdeaWise

How to Transform Your Ideas into Tomorrow's Innovations

STEVE RIVKIN

AND

FRASER SEITEL

JOHN WILEY & SONS, INC.

Published by John Wiley & Sons, Inc., New York.
Published simultaneously in Canada.

This publication is designed to provide accurate and authoritative information in
regard to the subject matter covered. It is sold with the understanding that the
publisher is not engaged in rendering professional services. If professional advice or
other expert assistance is required, the services of a competent professional person
should be sought.

Library of Congress Cataloging-in-Publication Data:

Rivkin, Steve, 1947–
    IdeaWise : how to transform your ideas into tomorrow's innovations / by Steve Rivkin
    and Fraser Seitel.
        p. cm.
    Includes index.
    ISBN 0-471-12956-9 (cloth : alk. paper)
    1. New products—Marketing.   I. Title: Transform your ideas into tomorrow's
    innovations.   II. Seitel, Fraser P.   III. Title.

    HF5415.153.R58 2001
    658.5'75—dc21   2001046852

Printed in the United States of America.

10 9 8 7 6 5 4 3 2 1

FOREWORD

During my 35-year career at The Chase Manhattan Bank, I was often exposed to ways by which the bank's performance could be improved and its profitability increased.

Bankers, by the very nature of their work, come across a vast array of business practices, both good and bad, and are in a unique position to assess how competitors in the same economic sector run their operations. The rigorous analysis of balance sheets, profit and loss statements, cash flow and other economic data, was, and is, the basis upon which credit is assessed and loans extended.

But, underneath the hard financial data are the practices—some call it the "corporate culture"—that separate the truly excellent companies from those that are simply good. These practices, which run the gamut from flexible work hours to corporate art programs to on-site day-care centers, are an invisible and intangible part of the bottom line, but they are there nevertheless. The really successful companies—GE, Microsoft, Intel—are well known for such innovative methods.

What I did not do as often as I should have as a bank CEO was to take the innovative ideas that I had observed around the world and introduce them at Chase. It would have made an immense difference. But, then, I did not have *IdeaWise* for a guide.

You, fortunately, don't have the same excuse.

Steve Rivkin and Fraser Seitel have provided an invaluable resource for business executives and entrepreneurs, as well as leaders in government and the not-for-profit sector. Humorous, insightful, and provocative are only a few of the words that come to mind to describe this superb book. It should be essential reading for anyone concerned about keeping his or her business or organization productive, expanding and dynamic.

DAVID ROCKEFELLER
Former Chairman and CEO
The Chase Manhattan Bank

CONTENTS

INTRODUCTION

Do you know how it feels to summon the muse . . . to sit cross-legged, yogalike, bathing in the warmth of divine inspiration . . . to climb to the mountaintop, to breathe in the cool air and compose, conceive, create?

Neither do we.

Frankly, most of us just aren't that creative. Oh sure, we come up with a good idea once in awhile, but even the Chicago Cubs once won the World Series . . . in 1908.

The sad truth is that if you're like us, you can't paint, act, play the piano, yodel, or even do card tricks. Can you ever expect, therefore, to be admired as a creative, dynamic, and, most of all, wise bastion of inspirational ideas?

You bet.

And this book will show you how.

How to become IdeaWise, that is.

Imagine for a moment that your task force was just asked to invent a new service. Or your advertising agency is competing for a new client. Or you've hit an organizational roadblock. Or your company wants to launch a new brand. Or last year's fund-raiser was a flop.

"Anybody got any ideas?"

How many times have you heard *that* during a meeting? How many times have you told yourself, "What I need here is a new idea"?

Say the words *new idea* and most people assume you're talking about a new product. After all, 26,000 new products were unveiled in the United States in the year 2000.

But, our definition of a new idea is broader.

A new idea is the result of fresh thinking, and it solves a problem. It's a novel notion that fuels tomorrow's success. It's anything that propels our business and professional lives.

Classic organizational thinking offers a six-step model for problem solving:

> 1. Define the problem.
> 2. Analyze potential causes.
> 3. **Identify possible solutions.**
> 4. Select the best solutions.
> 5. Develop an action plan.
> 6. Implement and evaluate the results.

Businesspeople are consumed with overanalyzing problems. But that's not what matters. *Solving* the problem is the real goal. That's the real capital in capitalism.

That's why Step Three is boldfaced. This book is all about Step Three because without solutions, you've got nothing.

When you become IdeaWise, you realize that the most creative, most innovative, and best ideas are right in front of you waiting to be noticed.

Frustrating their fruition is the knuckleheaded notion that true creativity springs miraculously from some internal spirit, or emerges mysteriously from some external muse.

Baloney.

What it really takes to innovate is a simple, singular, and solid commitment to unearth, stockpile, and focus on existing good ideas.

The search for a new idea isn't about reinventing the wheel.

Here's the shocking news, ladies and gentlemen: *It's okay to borrow an existing idea.* The genius comes in adapting it for your needs:

- What could you *adapt?* A hospital in Washington adapted a fund-raising idea from a charity in Florida, and it was the most successful fund-raiser in their history.

- What could you *substitute* in the approach, materials, ingredients, or appearance? That's how Shakespeare's *Romeo and Juliet* became *West Side Story.*

- What could you *combine* with an existing idea? That's why Band-Aids now are available with antibiotic ointment already on the pad.

- What could you *magnify* or *minimize?* McDonald's and Pizza Hut are shrinking their outlets to fit inside airport terminals.

- How could you put it to *other uses?* Arm & Hammer transformed baking soda into a refrigerator deodorant, an underarm deodorant, and a toothpaste ingredient.

- What could you *eliminate?* Saturn set out to get rid of the fear and loathing of salespeople in the car-buying process.

- What could you *reverse?* Toymaker Lego did an about-face on an ill-advised diversification and returned to its core business.

- What could you *bring back?* Commerce Bank brought back the old values of long hours and personal service in consumer and small business banking.

And the best news of all—you can do it!
Are you ready to borrow the best of existing ideas?
Read on. And you, too, will become IdeaWise.

CHAPTER

1

"But, I'm Not Creative"

Yes, you are. We all are.

You've just forgotten how to be creative. Or had it drilled out of you.

The truth is, we all have the ability to think in fresh ways and to solve problems.

A study of large groups of rank-and-file mechanics found that two-thirds of them rated above average in creative capacity.

Decades of psychological tests reveal that creative talent is normally distributed. All of us possess this talent to some degree.

What blocks the path to new ideas?

Sometimes, the blockage may build up because we lose the impulse to imagine as we grow up. Sometimes, bosses get in the way of original ideas. Sometimes, your own expectations are too high and get in your own way.

Kids Do It

We'll start by describing a consultation with real experts on this matter: Children.

We have a group of second graders sitting around their classroom, looking at an empty tin can with both ends cut off. Then, we ask them what they could use it for. Whoa, Nellie! The ideas come flying:

- A bug keeper.
- An ant home.
- A bank.
- To play kick the can.
- A washing machine for small people.
- A hat for a doll.
- A telephone.
- Half of stilts.
- A toy for the cat.
- A hand-squeezer for my dad.
- Something to melt down and morph into a Power Ranger.

Now, take that same empty tin can and give it to a group of upwardly mobile middle managers at any corporation in the United States.

"Please give me all possible uses for this empty tin can. You have 60 seconds."
Uhhhhhhhh.

What Happened?

For the most part, young people are open, trusting, un-self-conscious, and playful.

Parents, educators, and adults who want to become Idea-Wise, listen up. "Pretend" games are good. People should try lots of different things, without the pressure to succeed. Don't expect perfection in all things. Color outside the lines.

Original thinking has been described as an act of voluntary regression—a journey to an earlier psychological time.

Picasso once said that, after he learned to draw on a level with Raphael, he had to discover how to draw like a child.

How come kids are so clever? Why are adults less so?

Because our imagination tends to contract as our knowledge and judgment expand.

Original thinking has been described as an act of voluntary regression—a journey to an earlier psychological time.

Because the older we get, the less original and more standard our answers become.

Because the stubborn rules of business tend to stamp out fresh thinking.

What If?

When we were little kids, we all fantasized. We lived in castles filled with angels. A darkened room became a cave with knights and dragons. The legs of chairs became obstacles as we fought our way westward with the pioneers.

This is the "What if?" world of childhood.

If you retain that ability, or can regain it, you become what is typically called *creative*.

We've found that asking "What if?" becomes a lot easier when you attach that open-ended question to an existing idea. For example, What if we substituted an ingredient in this product? What if it were bigger? Or smaller? What if we combined something with the service we now offer?

Nahh, That Will Never Work

One big difference between children and adults is the level of criticism. Second graders usually don't get comments like these (all of which we've overheard at ideation sessions):

- Our customers would never go for that.
- Our employees would never go for that.
- We've tried that.
- That would take too much time.
- That would cost too much.
- Why don't you flesh that out in a memo?

- Maybe next year.
- That's not our job.
- Those people don't count.
- They'll never buy that.
- Who'd be interested in that?
- We don't have the time right now.
- That's not how we do things.

New ideas are fragile. They can be killed by a sneer or a yawn. But when we are children (or childlike), we don't harbor negativity. Instead, we wonder and explore simply for the joy of it. If you're in the business of encouraging new ideas, keep encouraging the people around you with a positive environment and avoid presenting worst-case scenarios.

If you're in the business of encouraging new ideas, keep encouraging the people around you with a positive environment and avoid presenting worst-case scenarios.

An Inborn Trait?

There's a misguided belief that the ability to come up with new ideas is an inborn trait and cannot be cultivated. In other words, either you are creative or you're not.

Baloney.

Too many people believe being creative is a gift limited to the very few and is associated only with uniqueness or artistry.

That highly intelligent people are the most creative. That creativity declines precipitously as you age.

More baloney. Decades of tests for creative aptitude have disproved every one of those beliefs.

That sudden hunch, that creative leap of the mind that "sees" in a flash how to solve a problem in a new way, is something quite different from general intelligence.

Studies reported in *Scientific American* show that people with a high "Eureka!" ability all have at least moderate intelligence. But beyond that, there seems to be no correlation between high intelligence and the ability to envision simple solutions for complex problems.

So here it is, flat out: Anybody can be creative:

- The Wright brothers were bike mechanics and school dropouts, not aeronautical engineers. (Education alone isn't the key to new ideas.)
- The ballpoint pen was invented by a sculptor. (Skilled people, trained in their field, don't have all the answers.)
- The telegraph was created by Samuel Morse, a professional portrait painter. (Artists can be technologists.)

Studies reported in **Scientific American** *show that people with a high "Eureka!" ability all have at least moderate intelligence. But beyond that, there seems to be no correlation between high intelligence and the ability to envision simple solutions for complex problems.*

So, Where Do New Ideas Come From?

Aristotle and Socrates pondered that question, without ever answering it. Since then, thousands of articles and books have been written about the creative process and the mind's inner workings. We have heard hundreds of theories and explanations, along with a large dose of mumbo jumbo.

Lateral thinking. Optimal visioning. Mind-brain interfaces. The neurophysiology of thought. Mental permeability. Conceptual fusioning. Whew!

An easy way to think about thinking is to frame it in three somewhat imprecise steps:

1. *Preparation.* Immerse yourself in the problem. Collect information, data, and opinions. Tell your brain to get to work.

2. *Incubation.* While you're busy doing other things, a part of your unconscious mind is swirling. Your brain juxtaposes thoughts and funnels concepts together.

3. *Illumination.* A new and reasonably complete idea surfaces, seemingly out of nowhere. Voilà! You've done it.

So, What's an Idea?

Those three steps are interesting—but they're not very helpful because they merely explain *what* happens, more or less. But, exactly *how* it happens is another matter.

So, let's consult another source of great wisdom in Western civilization—the comics. In the comic strip B.C., two characters are leaning on a rock, discussing our subject:

FIRST GUY: "What's an idea?"
SECOND GUY: "An idea is an inspirational thought."
FIRST GUY: "Where does it come from?"
SECOND GUY: "I haven't the slightest idea."

Ahhh, but there are Big Thinkers out there who would take issue with B.C.

They are absolutely, positively prepared to show you how to summon an inspirational thought. Lurking in the soft underbelly of American business, they make up the Idea Industry—a collection of self-righteous know-it-alls, modern-day Robin Hoods, and outright quacks.

They want to turn the search for new ideas into a gimmicky science.

It's a science, they maintain, that you will never fully master on your own.

But it's a science you can "rent" from this covey of ideation experts, for a significant piece of change.

Don't Buy the Idea Industry's Blather

The chimes.

The chimes.

The peaceful, restful, soothing chimes.

All is right with the world, here in the country, surrounded by rising sun, chirping birds, and eager coworkers.

It is the stroke of eight. Let the brainstorming session begin.

Welcome to Sherman Forest everybody. My name is Buddy Boffstrom, and I'll be your BrainStem leader. Today, we're going to be thinking, as we like to call it at BrainStem LLC. and in the idea generation business generally, "out of the box."

Our mission is simple. By the end of the day, we will have come up with a revolutionary new lug nut—an innovation about which Zockenfluster Corporation can be proud.

And you 23 managers are going to come up with that innovation. I know you may be dubious. But trust me.

Let's start by breaking the ice. I'd like everybody to get up and tell me about your most embarrassing moment in a locker room. Then, we'll meditate, levitate, and concentrate on the question, "If I were a lug nut, to which component of a subcompact car would I most like to affix myself?"

Welcome to every middle manager's darkest nightmare, "the Offsite Idea Generation Retreat."

It is guaranteed to addle the brain, frazzle the nerves, and make the attendees want to hide in the lower regions of their resort hotel.

Not to worry. Your trepidation isn't unusual. Battery-recharging retreats often make great sense. But when it comes to coming up with new products, new business strategies, new management approaches, new marketing campaigns, or new ideas generally—most of the seminars, retreats, books, and courses offer more heat than light.

The problem can be summarized in one dreaded word, *consultants*.

Beware Consultant-Speak

Certainly there are consultants who add value and outside perspective and important insights that management should consider. (Hey, we're consultants ourselves, and we're not chopped liver!) But . . . and this is a big *but* . . . many consultants are charlatans, pretenders, or snake oil salesmen, with their own odd jargon and even stranger ideas. No wonder Rupert Murdoch labels the consulting advice he receives regularly as "fairly obvious." And even Tom Peters, a consultant's consultant, has candidly acknowledged that American industry's love affair with consultants is an example of managers "getting suckered in by people like me."

What is obvious to Murdoch and Peters apparently escapes most of their colleagues in corporate America. In a business climate where technology and competition have inspired most organizations to become meaner and leaner with internal resources, the desire to find that cutting-edge external guru has intensified.

"In Search of Suckers" is how *Fortune* magazine described the quest for new wave consultants, "armed with nothing more than pens, podiums, and tremendous shamelessness."

In a business climate where technology and competition have inspired most organizations to become meaner and leaner with internal resources, the desire to find that cutting-edge external guru has intensified.

In few areas are the shamelessness—or the stakes—higher than in the so-called idea industry:

- One self-professed consulting genius charges corporate clients up to $1 million for one "Big Idea."
- One $100 billion bank CEO spent millions of dollars and thousands of hours of management time on a guru who promised to lead the company's "vision quest" for a new

identity. Sure enough, they got it. After completion of the sessions—and payment of the fee—the bank was sold to another bank, and the CEO was demoted by his new boss.

- In the area of employee training alone, American business spends $15 billion annually. The fastest-growing segment? Personal transformation and self-improvement, part and parcel of the Idea Industry.

Date with Destitution

For only $8,995 (airfare not included), you could spend eight days with personal transformation guru Tony Robbins on his Fiji hideaway, with 59 other potential idea generators, in what the 6 foot 6 inch motivational counselor called his "Date with Destiny" program.

Now some people swear by the ever-affable Robbins. "I wouldn't spend this kind of money if I didn't believe," said one Robbins graduate, a real estate broker who climbed a 60-foot pole and walked through fire, on his own Date with Destiny.

And we've got nothing against Tony Robbins (he's a lot bigger than we are, after all, and we're inveterate cowards).

But we do find troubling what the Tony Robbinses, Zig Ziglars, Fran Tarkentons, Pat Reillys, Lou Holtzes, and Tom Peterses and all the other eminently persuasive Pollyannas have wrought on American business.

Specifically, they've introduced—and worse, sold—the false notion that the weirder the presenter . . . the more unlikely the premise . . . the more absurd the concept . . . then, the greater the prospect of coming up with a new successful business idea.

That's why these kinds of scenes are typical:

- Boeing gathers top managers, asks them to put all their bad company experiences on paper, and then burn the paper in a ritual act of corporate death and rebirth.

- Honeywell sends executives to the desert of New Mexico to study the traditions of the Apache and Navajo, including the Medicine Wheel, a representation of the human experience.

- A Georgetown University business school professor requires students to go out on campus in broad daylight and scream at the top of their lungs. Alternatively, they can pretend they're a slice of pizza or a bowl of Jell-O, or if they are less ambitious, they can bark like a dog.

Managers aren't stupid. Eventually, they realize the utter sham of such balderdash. One Bain & Company survey of 4,000 executives, for example, showed that a whopping 77 percent said that the management tools they were sold promised more than they delivered.

No matter how much companies fork over for mind pumping, mood morphing, Nerf ball battles, and meditative chanting—the cold truth is that the Idea Industry's emperors have no clothes.

No matter how much companies fork over for mind pumping, mood morphing, Nerf ball battles, and meditative chanting—the cold truth is that the Idea Industry's emperors have no clothes.

Fruit of the Loon

What business wreckage, you may ask, has the Idea Industry wrought?

Plenty.

The erstwhile "New Economy" is littered with the carcasses of out-of-the-box, innovative concepts that in the end proved to be deader than Mussolini, to the ultimate financial horror of millions of chastened investors (two of whom, alas, wrote this book):

- Pets.com was the answer to every animal lover's prayers—an Internet site from which they could order everything from Fido's gourmet nibbles and canine accessories to, well, Fido himself. In a masterstroke of inventiveness, the company adopted a doglike sock puppet as its advertising spokesperson. The pet store/shop-by-Net concept made great sense, except for one small undetected wild card—competition. Lots of it. From neighborhood pet stores to megamall pet stores to other pet stores on the Internet itself. There were also little operational hurdles, like having to absorb the whopping shipping costs for 50-pound sacks of dog chow.

- Cyberianoutpost.com was a similar project, with equally high hopes. What Outpost offered was the opportunity to purchase cut-rate computers and related supplies, via (ready for this?) the Internet! Sheer genius. And the company got even more inventive than its Net pet store counterpart when it sought to reach as far out-of-the-box as possible in its advertising. *Specifically,* Cyberianoutpost.com TV ads highlighted a football field full of marching band members being attacked by rats. The significance of this to a Web computer seller was clear. Huh? And even more cleverly, the company chose to subtly advertise its message during $1 million-a-minute Super Bowl broadcasts. Until, that is, the money ran out.

- DrKoop.com was fronted by the easily recognized former Surgeon General C. Everett Koop. The brilliance of DrKoop.com was its availability at all hours to dispense medical advice over the Internet. Such a concept, reasoned the venture capitalists and assorted new age business geniuses who came up with the idea, was that the name recognition and credibility of Dr. Koop would draw millions of people, and therefore millions of sponsorship dollars, to the site. Good thinking. What they failed to consider, however, was that a plethora of similarly constituted Web sites would spring up offering even more learned medical advice. Not to mention the competition offered by local clinics and doctors, who actually might know something about a patient's particular ailment.

In the end the Pets.com sock puppet shriveled into Chapter 11 bankruptcy . . . the Cyberianoutpost.com rats deserted the sinking ship . . . and even Dr. Koop cashed in his stock options and flew the, well, coop.

The Age of Innovation

Just because you can't trust consultants (or at least, *some* consultants) doesn't mean you can afford to throw out the innovation baby with the consultant bath water. You simply must innovate.

It has become commonplace to call the era in which we live, "The Information Age." But "The Innovation Age" is more like it.

Every year, the U.S. Patent and Trademark Office receives upward of 250,000 patent applications—a steady 15 percent annual increase in the number of patents on record. While not all patents mean new products, the steadily rising number indicates that many companies have gotten the message.

And that message is—innovate or die, or at least wither.

Sure, there's no way to recession-proof an organization. And when the broad economy hits the skids, such as it did in 2001, a falling tide rocks all the boats.

But good companies—the General Electrics and Texas Instruments and IBMs of the world—have recognized that constant innovation gives them a better chance to hold their own in falling economies and a head start (not to mention leg up) when the economic clouds lift.

It has become commonplace to call the era in which we live, "The Information Age." But "The Innovation Age" is more like it.

For years, IBM has been the annual leader in winning new U.S. patents. The company now receives about 3,000 new patents a year, and recently, that number has increased by 50 percent per annum.

Any correlation between IBM's perpetual push for new products and the company's stellar stock market performance, even in bad times? Absolutely.

Consider China

Innovation spurs economic activity and enhances productivity. Put simply, innovation creates the wealth on which people and societies depend. It has been this way since civilization began:

- The Greeks, among other things, produced the lever, wedge, pulley, and gear for transportation, manufacturing, and distribution purposes.
- Societies of the Middle Ages developed the horseshoe and stirrup, which revolutionized mobility, warfare, and conquest.
- Islam produced paper, which was a lot easier to write on than rocks, and accelerated communication.
- The Chinese, as technologically sophisticated as any early society, invented matches, the umbrella, and the tooth-brush, among scores of other innovations.

But consider China.

Before 1400, the Chinese were literally the most advanced civilization on earth. Before Columbus was a gleam in Queen Is-abella's eye, the Chinese were dispatching gargantuan "treasure ships" with crews of 500, to the farthest reaches of the Persian Gulf and East Africa. Their mission was to explore, prospect, and plunder (mostly plunder) the natural wealth of these far-away lands.

China's navigational invention and innovation were profound. Had they kept going, the Chinese likely would have pioneered the Industrial Revolution, colonized Europe, and invented Starbucks.

But Chinese innovation didn't keep going. It stopped, dead in its tracks, blocked by a burgeoning bureaucracy that focused on public welfare. They built walls, not wealth. And the innovative technological entrepreneurship that had paced China's early expansion was sacrificed and lost.

Waiting eagerly on the sidelines, ready and willing to receive the crown jewel of innovation from China, was Western civilization. And it has safeguarded this wealth-building, society-sustaining jewel ever since.

What Have You Done for Me Lately?

Today, consumers—even consumers in China—want more and want better and want it now.

As a consequence:

- In the United States 70 percent of overall growth is achieved through new product development.
- U.S. companies spend more than $250 billion each year on research and development.

- Copyrighted material contributes more than $400 billion to the nation's economy and is our single most important export.

Companies must have new products and services for earnings growth. And they must attract the very best people (most everyone would rather work for a "winner").

The good news from all this is that U.S. firms devote 8 to 16 percent of their net revenues each year on new and better products. The bad news, though, is that 65 percent of these new products are deader than Mussolini within 12 months.

Constant innovation is a constant challenge for any organization that wishes to remain a leader.

Constant innovation is a constant challenge for any organization that wishes to remain a leader.

Stated another way, in an Age of Instant Gratification and equally Instant Rejection, of media onslaughts 24 hour a day, seven days a week; of Internet shopping, online chat rooms, and a mobile phone in every pocket; where the largest SUV or latest Palm Pilot or living room sound system is the one and only first new choice—firms that seek to survive must live to innovate.

If It Ain't Broke, Break It

For every IBM or Intel, GE, or Texas Instruments seeking constantly to push the envelope, challenge what they do, and devise new innovative solutions for what already works, the business landscape is littered with countless others who got too smug, too cute, or too cocky for their own good.

In the twenty-first century, corporate cockiness is deader than you-know-who.

The sad case of Xerox is a powerful example.

Not only was Xerox "the copier company," but Xerox literally meant "copy." The two words became synonymous.

"Would you Xerox that for me," was the standard request. "Give me 10 Xeroxes of that invoice and put them on my desk."

Xerox had cornered the market. Others would kill for such a leadership position.

But Xerox, the company, wasn't so pleased about the recognition.

"You can't Xerox a Xerox on a Xerox," the company smugly admonished in its advertising, reminding one and all that Xerox was a trademarked corporate name and should not be mistaken for a run-of-the-mill verb, suggesting the act of duplicating paper.

And there Xerox stood, at the apex of the copying business, for a long time. Too long, as it turned out. Over time, complacency set in. Xerox failed to challenge itself, failed to question the assumptions that underpinned its business.

Until it was too late.

Today, after several late, failed attempts at reinvention, Xerox is a shadow of its former self. Its business and its balance sheet have been shattered, its new management has been scrapped, and its franchise and its credibility have been sapped.

The once proud Xerox company clings to corporate life and struggles to survive. What wouldn't it give today to hear someone, anyone, ask, "Xerox a copy of this for me"?

Enough Already!

All right, you get the point.

Paying lots of stockholder equity to a modern muse, who guarantees to inspire you with new ideas, usually doesn't work.

Save your money for more worthwhile corporate purposes.

But . . . and this is another big *but* . . . don't abandon the search for new ideas. That would be suicidal.

Don't think for a moment that just because you've done things the same way for years and just because you're good at your job and just because the organization is humming along that you don't need to come up with new services or new systems or new programs.

Corporations, as the economists say and as anyone from Lee Iacocca to Jack Welch to Bill Gates will affirm, must be managed "to operate in perpetuity."

Which means, *forever.* That's why people buy a company's products, invest in its stock, or join it as employees.

Don't think for a moment that just because you've done things the same way for years and just because you're good at your job and just because the organization is humming along that you don't need to come up with new services or new systems or new programs.

And the only way to ensure that services remain relevant, jobs continue to make sense, or that organizations continue to be viable, is to keep coming up with new and better ideas.

Trumpeting Schumpeter

"Businessmen go down with their businesses because they like the old way so well they cannot bring themselves to change," said Henry Ford in *My Life and Work* in 1922.

Lucent. Xerox. CMGI. iVillage. eToys. Priceline.com.

Oh, the ignominy.

From the debris of all the dot-bombs, liquidations, layoffs, bankruptcies, shattered stocks, and splattered corporate carcasses of the initial years of the twenty-first century a new, old hero has emerged: the 1930s Austrian economist Joseph Schumpeter.

He coined the term *creative destruction,* to signify that capitalism is renewed only when the old and tired and inflexible companies are destroyed, thus clearing the path for the emergence of new and vibrant companies with fresh ideas and creative thinking.

So that's the choice: You can be either destroyer or destroyee.

To achieve the former and escape the latter requires inspiration, imagination, innovation. In other words: new ideas.

So that's the choice: You can be either destroyer or destroyee.

And how do you come up with them? We thought you'd never ask.

3

Seek and Ye Shall Find

New ideas are out there, like ripened fruit on a tree. But they don't miraculously fall into your basket. You must exert some effort to fill it up with ideas.

Are you going to trek up some mountain, surround yourself with beads and feathers, and chant until—Eureka!—a fully-formed brainstorm appears? (That's a waste of boot leather.)

The Wisdom of Yogi

Better to follow the wisdom of Yogi Berra: "You can observe a lot just by watchin'."

Simple? Sure it is. Trite? Maybe. But too few of us—and too few of our companies—take the time to look and see anything.

The problem with the way most of us think is that we don't pay enough attention to the all-important first step of *perception* in coming up with new information. We're always in a rush to reach Step Two, the processing of what we perceive.

We repeat: The most creative, most innovative ideas are right there, in front of you.

You can observe and watch in one of two basic ways:

1. By accident, by chance, by serendipity. (The key is collecting the ideas in some retrievable way.)

2. By systematically seeking out an answer that you instinctively know exists. (But where is it?)

We repeat: The most creative, most innovative ideas are right there, in front of you.

Sweet Serendipity

The word serendipity means the ability to make fortunate discoveries by accident. (The characters in a Persian fairy tale *The Three Princes of Serendip* made such discoveries, and the word wove its way into English.)

• Carlos Gutierrez, the CEO of cereal giant Kellogg, goes looking for new ideas. He reads *People* to stay in tune with pop culture. He attends Matchbox 20 concerts with his teenage kids. He's a nut about baseball.

Will any of this guarantee a new idea for his food business? Of course not. But, visiting your customers where they live is one way to open yourself up to new information, and maybe stumble across a new idea.

- Thomas Stemberg, the founder of Staples, believes in seeing the world at ground level. He shops his stores like a customer. He asks questions that a customer would ask, like "Where can I find printer cartridge number 6534?"

Gutierrez and Stemberg are both following in the footsteps of a business legend. Alfred P. Sloan, who built General Motors into the world's leading manufacturing entity in the 1930s, defied the typical notion of a chairman because he liked to work personally with customers.

There's gold down there in the mud of the marketplace.

Every so often, Sloan would disappear from Detroit headquarters and show up at a dealer's lot in another city. He would introduce himself and ask the dealer's permission to work as an assistant service manager, or as a salesman, for a few days. (No surprise, the dealers always said yes.) The next week, Sloan would be back in Detroit, firing off memos on customer behavior and customer preferences toward everything from dealers to auto styling.

There's gold down there in the mud of the marketplace. Peter Drucker, the high priest of management thinking, has argued that by working regularly in the field, Sloan spotted more trends and more important trends than did customer re-search—and spotted them earlier.

Sloan observed. And he acted on what he saw.

Going for a Ride

Wal-Mart founder Sam Walton, the richest man in the United States when he died, used to go for delivery rides with Wal-Mart truckers. He told colleagues it was a lot of fun. But just imagine how much he learned from those rides.

The unpretentious "Mister Sam" definitely liked to join his troops in the trenches. Once when he was restless in the middle of the night, he got out of bed, got dressed, and drove to an all-night bakery, where he bought dozens of doughnuts. He took them down to the loading dock of one of his stores and spent the night talking to the crews. While he was there, he learned that this crew needed more shower stalls, so he took care of it himself the next morning. This was when sales were around the $25 billion level.

Enlisting the Enlisted

Michael Abrashoff is the commander of the *USS Benfold*, a Navy destroyer in the Pacific fleet. Before he took command of the ship, he had held a desk job at the Pentagon. Once aboard the *Benfold*, he took his concept of leadership down to the front lines, or rather, brought the front lines to him. He invited each of the enlisted men and women into his private quarters and asked these questions: "What do you like about the *Ben-fold?* What don't you like about it? What would you change?"

Question: ***Are you spending time "below decks" with your troops?***

Results? More than $1 million in savings from the crew's suggestions, some of the best morale in the Navy, and an award as the best ship in the fleet. All of this was based on ideas that would never have seen the light of day if Commander Abrashoff hadn't looked—and listened—below decks.

Question: Are you spending time "below decks" with your troops?

Start Looking

So, get out of your Herman Miller Aeron chair and go take a walk in the world:

- You wander the aisles of a Wal-Mart, thinking about their obsessive attention to customers' needs. Pretty soon, you're watching an elderly shopper looking at price labels large enough for her to read without bifocals. (*A minor detail? How easy is it to read all the paper your business produces?*)

- You notice a car rental company is celebrating its anniversary by rolling back prices for one day to long-ago levels. And getting lots of publicity in the process. (*Does your business have an anniversary coming up?*)

- You observe two hospitals that are ready to celebrate the fifth year of their merger. Instead of stuffy speeches and self-serving congratulations, they throw a big outdoor birthday party for all the five-year-olds in the county. TV news trucks roll in from surrounding markets to film an acre of frolicking kids. The hospital wheels out a gigantic, Guinness-record-worthy cake fashioned in the shape of the digit five. The competitor of the merged hospitals is apoplectic. After all, many of those kids were babies birthed at its facility. (*Why does your company always celebrate milestones in the same old stuffy manner?*)

Stockpile Those Ideas

Did something tickle your fancy while you were out on your walk searching for ideas?

- Einstein wrote down his thoughts.
- Edison sketched his ideas in detail.
- Da Vinci filled notebooks with his musings.
- Guy Caron is the founder of the National Circus School in Montreal, and is artistic director of the famed Cirque du Soleil. For inspiration for his avant-garde shows, he keeps a notebook filled with clippings and photographs, images that range from cartoons to Magritte paintings. He gives these to a team of people who help bring his ideas to life. For music for the same shows, he jots down pieces from more than 1,500 CDs in his collection. The result for a recent show named *Dralion* (an amalgam of "dragon" and

"lion") was a fusion of sounds from Andalusia, Africa, Central Europe, and the West.

The point is, these creative people all collected their ideas. You should do the same. Start a journal, a clipping file, a computer file, for those nifty notions you come across.

Have you ever had a brilliant idea in the middle of the night that faded into a hazy recollection by 7 A.M.? Keep a pad by the bed, a voice recorder in the car.

"Those thoughts that come unsought," said Francis Bacon, "are commonly the most valuable, and should be secured, because they seldom return."

Some people say their best ideas have come to them in the bathtub or shower. (Yes, there are waterproof pencils and writing tablets.)

Memory is not a tape recorder that stores information when we turn it on. Seeing is not akin to photographing the world, crisply registering an image.

Write it down. Log it on your laptop. Plop it into your palmtop. Just keep that possible idea somewhere. Don't trust your memory.

Write it down. Log it on your laptop.
Plop it into your palmtop.
Just keep that possible idea somewhere.
Don't trust your memory.

Within 24 hours, say memory experts, we forget 80 percent of what we think we have learned. (We may repeat those statistics in a later chapter in case you have forgotten.)

A Manager for All Seasons

Let's say you're on an airplane, catching up on your reading, going through mail, trade journals, and magazines. Somewhere in that pile, in a business magazine you don't always look at, you come across an article about Joe Torre, the manager of the New York Yankees.

It catches your attention because, number one, you're a baseball fan. Number two, you're curious about the writer's premise that Joe Torre is actually a model for today's corporate managers because he gets the most out of his workers, keeps a demanding boss happy, and delivers a stream of winners. As you read on, you find yourself intrigued by some of Joe's management principles:

- *Dump the motivational speeches to the team.* (He relies instead on frequent one-on-ones that he attunes to the psyches of individual players.)
- *Remind everybody of their importance.* (He makes even bit players feel useful.)
- *Don't punish failure.* (He stays loyal to slumping players, creating a positive paradox where failure is tolerated in the glare of a high-performance workplace.)

Now you're revved up because you see a bunch of applications for these ideas—starting with a speech you have to write for the new divisional CEO, who has promised a brave new way of running his operation.

Hey, you just have to remember a few key ideas from Joe Torre. You can do that, right?

Here's what will happen. Unless you highlight that article immediately . . . unless you take notes for yourself right now . . . unless you put it in a file devoted to that speech right now . . . it will all turn to dust before you work your way through the rest of your reading pile. Don't trust your memory.

Primacy and Recency

A simple exercise will prove the point. Read the following list of words just once. Do not study them. Just read each one to yourself in order. Then, close the book and write down as many of the words as you can, in whatever order they occur to you:

> fingerprint, piston, penis, jelly, stoplight, lawnmower, silk, dream, champagne, flowers, blindfold, puddle, terrorist, mailbox, shampoo, saucer, jeans, penguin, townhouse, lottery, heaven

Because there are more than seven words, you probably did not remember them all. (Sixty years ago, Harvard psychologist George Miller found that only seven pieces of information— like seven brands in a category, or seven digits in a phone number—can easily be held in short-term memory.) But you did remember some of the words. There is a *primacy* and a *recency* effect taking place. You were more likely to remember a word at the beginning of the list, and at the end of the list.

The reason for the primacy effect is that you had a clean mental slate when you began. The reason for the recency effect is that there was less interference between the words at the end of the list and the recall time than between the words in the middle of the list and the recall time:

- During a college lecture, students best remember material presented at the start of the class and at the end, but their recall dips drastically in the middle.
- If you are speaking at a business meeting and want to make a point that people will really remember, make it either early or late.

Back to that interesting article about Joe Torre. Unless you were fortunate enough to read that article right after you buckled into Seat 10C . . . or much later, just as you were landing . . . good luck in remembering its key points. (Good luck in even remembering what magazine it was in!)

That's why effective people stockpile their ideas.

Seek and Ye Shall Find

We once sat down with a group of hospital executives and medical staff leaders, and asked where they could use some new ideas.

They didn't talk much about new products or services. What they wanted were answers to operational problems and people issues:

- How do we provide care for people living just outside our service area?

- How do we recruit more family practice doctors to our community?

- How do we reduce the workforce without crippling morale?

- How do we increase employee turnout at a town meeting with the CEO?

- How do we get our MDs and DOs to spend more time with each other?

- How can we develop a more equitable weekend rotation schedule at our clinic?

You want answers? You can get answers! Somebody, somewhere probably already has looked for what you are looking for. So to prove the point, let's help these nice health care folks identify what's worked for someone else.

The Service Area Question

We'll use the hospital executives' first question on the preceding list as our illustration: *How do we provide care for people living just outside our service area?*

To begin with, you should go to the survey journals that summarize information in the field. (Every business has a publication or database modeled on the *Reader's Digest's* concept of abstracting existing material.)

In the hospital management arena, there is COR Healthcare Resources. Each month, it scans thousands of articles to produce newsletters on health care management methods.

Within their archives, you are likely to find examples of how some of the 5,000 U.S. hospitals have addressed this issue. Yep, you just landed on a treatise titled "Importance of Medical Center Outreach in Serving the Population of Rural Eastern Kentucky." Now, your job is to borrow and adapt.

Internet Intelligence

The knockout punch in finding ideas is the Internet, which is an astounding compilation of information at your fingertips. That's the good news.

The bad news is that the Internet is an ocean of unedited, unreliable data, lacking filters, editors, or any pretense of accuracy; it's a place where 15-year-old boys can successfully masquerade as hotshot lawyers.

But let's give our hospital managers the benefit of the doubt. Let's assume they are comfortable using various search engines and portals, and are familiar with computer logic. And, they are skilled enough to separate wheat from chaff.

A diligent search would yield multiple ideas on community outreach. Here's just one, from St. Luke's Hospital in Bethlehem, Pennsylvania: a mobile health van designed to take the hospital's preventive services to residents who can't or won't come to the hospital itself. Your reservoir is suddenly full of good stuff about St. Luke's development and management of their "HealthStar" van:

- The most desirable services to offer (asthma screenings, parenting programs, HIV/AIDS prevention, nutrition, etc.).

- Obtaining funds and budgeting for the van's operations.
- Recruiting and training drivers.
- Procuring signage for a 35-foot vehicle.
- Scheduling neighborhood routes.
- Connecting with health fairs and other community events.
- Mobilizing press attention.

No need to reinvent the wheel. You've got a complete dossier on one good way to reach out to the community.

Was this a staggeringly creative exercise? A breakthrough new notion of epic proportions? Or was it simply the acquisition of a powerful, pragmatic blueprint that the hospital could put to work immediately? You be the judge.

Get a Grip

Information on almost everything is already out there.

Let's say you're toiling away at LeadingEdge ImageWorks. Your job is to design a new bottle for a new beverage. And, you've just loaded a nifty new design program into your Power Mac G4. Man oh man, you've got computing power for three billion calculations per second! With that kind of velocity, you'll have a zillion design concepts before the boss even asks how . . .

Hold on, Picasso. Why don't you first redirect all that computing muscle into a search engine? You'll quickly learn that scientists have studied microscopically the ergonomics of bottles; that behaviorists have videotaped people drinking their beverages and have made plaster casts of their hands; that researchers even know how big a big gulp really is (6.44 ounces).

Information on almost everything is already out there.

All that wisdom might lead you toward a sleeker, curvier new design. (After Gatorade introduced a bigger hourglass-shaped plastic bottle, sales jumped as much as 25 percent in some areas.)

It's all there, if you just look for it.

Information Experts

In your company, you are probably the decision maker, not the information expert. So, if you (or your assistant or your secretary, if you're blessed with either) cannot find a decent answer in 15 minutes of online searching, then call a halt to the search.

You're better off asking a librarian, a professional freelance researcher, or information clearinghouse to do the job:

- Never hesitate to ask questions in a public library. Professional librarians are paid to answer them. That's their job. If they can't answer a question, they can tell you who might or can lead you to another source.

- Hundreds of libraries are devoted to business affairs, and other specialized topics. Reference librarians, in either a public or academic library, can guide you through their section of encyclopedias, compendiums, and directories.

- Niche publications and associations are dandy sources of information for almost any interest or topic. There are several excellent directories of thousands of publications, and titles for most of them are free at MediaFinder.com. Three excellent sources for associations and organizations are the *Encyclopedia of Associations*, the *National Directory of Trade and Professional Organizations*, and *AssociationCentral.com*.

- If you work in a corporate setting, there's usually some department that is information-rich: Corporate Communications, Public Relations, Marketing Communications, Investor Relations, or, ideally, the Company Library.

- There are also companies made up of information specialists who search out answers for a living. Some specialize in one industry, such as pharmaceuticals. Others are generalists. These people charge by the hour, by the project, or by a monthly retainer. You'll find listings for information specialists in directories of information brokers and competitive intelligence brokers.

Raw Material

Enchantment Resort is a swank, New Age destination in Sedona, Arizona, one of the top 15 resorts in the United States, according to the readers of *Travel & Leisure*. When the resort built a separate luxury spa, it decided to name the spa in honor of the Native Americans whose ancestral homes are carved into the surrounding canyon walls. A search through the dictionaries and mythology of the Apache and the Yavapai produced the name *Mii Amo*, which means "forward movement." (Seek and ye shall find.)

In a world with a gazillion gigabytes of information, always assume that if an answer exists, it's yours for the asking:

- The boss taps you to chair a task force on a possible collaboration with Throckmorton Sprockets, a one-time competitor. A week ago, you could barely spell collaboration. Now you're wondering, *What makes for a successful versus an unsuccessful collaboration—and where the heck do I find out?* No problem. An 80-year-old Midwestern research institute literally wrote the handbook on collaboration. (PS: There are 19 factors that influence successful collaborations.)

- You're the brand manager for a new salad dressing that overflows with herbs and spices from the Mediterranean. You need a name. You think of Kraft's famous Catalina brand and thus Catalina Island and wonder, *Maybe we could use the name of an island in the Mediterranean. There must be hundreds. But where . . . ?* No problem. Your atlas has a list. The Internet has a longer list.

In a world with a gazillion gigabytes of information, always assume that if an answer exists, it's yours for the asking.

- You're a major employer in San Bernardino County, which has a higher percentage of Hispanic residents (33 percent) than the state of California as a whole (29 percent). Problem is, your emporium is considered inaccessible, inhospitable to the Hispanic community. You wonder, *How have other businesses coped with this phenomenon? ¿Necesita mas información? No hay problema.*

It doesn't matter how or where you find that ripened fruit. The point is, there's now fruit in your basket and ideas galore in hand. The goal remains the same. You want something that could solve a problem or fuel tomorrow's success. Now that you've got your fruit, you're ready to make an innovation cocktail.

Thomas Edison Was Right

If there's one thing that Americans love, it's frozen desserts. Consumption of ice cream continues to grow, year after year; in the year 2000 it reached 1.6 billion gallons.

But the folks at Häagen-Dazs were concerned. They weren't scooping up enough sales at the premium end of the market. What to do? The corporate objective was to stimulate sales with a new ice cream flavor.

The challenge? Invent that delicious new flavor.

Now, the traditional route to corporate ice cream creativity would mean a planning retreat in a warm climate for the marketing team. There they would have a chance to lap up ice cream lore, and to ask each other such intriguing questions as,

If I were the color magenta in a box of Crayola crayons, what would I taste like?

Then, they could commission a roomful of chefs to whip up exotic flavors. Follow that up with thousands of taste tests with consumers across the land.

Investment: 12 months, hundreds of thousands of dollars. Results: Dubious.

Or, Häagen-Dazs could ask one simple question: What is the best-selling flavor we have outside the United States? The answer came from Buenos Aires: *Dulce de Leche,* named after a wildly popular caramelized mix of sugar and whole milk. The company took that existing flavor worldwide. Now, in the United States, only vanilla sells better. Dulce de Leche is doing $1 million a month in revenues.

Show Me Someone Else's Idea

Learn what Häagen-Dazs learned. When you're IdeaWise, the best ideas are borrowed ideas.

That's not only the simplest way to solve a problem, it's also the best.

Thomas Edison said:

> Make it a habit to be on the lookout for novel and interest-ing ideas that others have used successfully. Your idea needs to be original only in its adaptation to the problem you are currently working on.

Thank you, Professor, for blessing the act of borrowing.

Okay, so we're being polite. We're really talking about copying, filching, pilfering, sponging, and basically stealing an existing idea.

When you're IdeaWise, the best ideas are borrowed ideas.

So what? Just follow Edison's great guidance and you're on safe ground. The genius is in adapting someone else's solution to your problem:

- *In war.*   During the American Revolution, the Minutemen scored their first major victory by adapting a strategy previously used against them by Indians during the French and Indian War. Minutemen sniped at massed English troops from behind stone walls and trees. (Today, we'd call it guerrilla warfare.) In the 1770s, it was a radical departure for white men to use this Indian tactic. The European style had been frontal volleys—you know, line up directly across from each other and just blast away. To the British, this divergence from the standard rules of engagement was vicious and cowardly. Adapting this successful fighting idea allowed the Americans to seize an early advantage in the war.

- *In communication.*   Samuel Morse was trying to figure out how to produce a telegraphic signal strong enough to transmit coast to coast. One day he saw stablehands substituting fresh horses for tired horses at a relay station. His adaptation was to give the signal a periodic boost of power.

- *In medicine.*   Dr. Rene Laennec was looking for a way to help diagnose his patients. He was inspired to invent the stethoscope when he observed children sending signals to each other by tapping on either end of a hollow log.

- *In your own company.*   Häagen-Dazs stole from its own Southern Hemisphere operations. Is that a crime? A market development manager at 3M Canada identified a market for systems that would allow library visitors to check out books without assistance. As she worked toward a prototype, she discovered (at a library association meeting) that 3M Australia had been working on a similar product. Minds and budgets merged. Today, SelfCheck is one of the main products in the portfolio of 3M Library Systems.

- *In the same industry.*   Michael O'Leary is CEO of Ryanair, a regional European airline he rebuilt a decade ago on the no-frills model of Southwest Airlines. Did his borrowed idea take off? Ryanair now flies to 55 destinations in Ireland (its home base), France, Germany, Italy, Denmark, Norway, and Sweden. Revenues in 2001 were $427 million; net income was $91 million. It is one of the only thriving European carriers.

Famous Borrowers Are Everywhere

The search for an elusive, breakthrough idea is exactly that—*elusive.* The best ideas are borrowed ideas. If you're IdeaWise, you'll find yourself in the company of many famous borrowers.

As Dale Carnegie once wrote:

The ideas I stand for are not mine. I borrowed them from Socrates. I swiped them from Chesterfield. I stole them from Jesus. And I put them in a book. If you don't like their rules, whose would you use?

If you're IdeaWise, you'll find yourself in the company of many famous borrowers.

Like Mr. Carnegie, Leopoldo Fernandez Pujals also liked somebody else's rules—namely, Domino's Pizza and their home delivery idea. As more women began entering the workforce in Spain, this Cuban American marketer sensed Spain's growing appetite for fast food. So he invested $80,000 to start a pizza delivery service in Madrid. Now, TelePizza boasts $294 million in sales, employs 13,000 workers, and has 760 outlets in eight countries.

Inspiration from Paris

Andy Garvin liked what he found in Paris.

Working for *Newsweek* magazine there, and assigned to write a story on Marcel Bich, founder of the Bic Corporation, Garvin needed quick background information. He did what all the magazine's Paris staffers did—he picked up the phone and dialed SVP.

SVP (for *s'il vous plait,* or "if you please" in French) was a fixture in French business affairs. It was founded in a straightforward premise: When your business has a question, we find the answer.

Andy Garvin is the son and grandson of successful entrepreneurs. The lightbulb went on: He could borrow this French concept and take it to the United States. So, Garvin soaked up details about SVP's operations. He came back to New York with figures, methods, and a licensing deal.

The SVP concept works because the information that most organizations need already exists. (How much lamb did New Zealand export last year? Can you explain COBRA in everyday language? What's the potential market for digital widgets? That sort of thing.)

Even with the Internet, finding the information can be a hassle. People don't always know where to look or what source to trust. Plus, they're in a hurry.

The company Andy Garvin founded—Find/SVP—began as a two-person office with six shelf feet of reference materials. Today his borrowed idea is a $24 million, publicly traded enterprise with more than 100 employee consultants.

Inspiration from Sweden

Survivor was the runaway smash of two consecutive TV seasons. How did the show's creators outwit, outplay, and outlast other shows to top the ratings?

Simple. They borrowed the concept from a hit Swedish TV program called *Expedition Robinson.* (Which was transformed into *Castaway* in England.)

Borrowing is an honored practice on the tube. *Whose Line Is It Anyway?* a surprise hit for ABC, was a direct lift from a British program of the same name. Remember *All in the Family* with the irascible Archie Bunker? This American classic was adapted from a British TV staple called *Til Death Do Us Part.*

Dick Wolf, the creator of TV's *Law & Order* and other successful shows, has said there are no new ideas in television, there is only execution.

Inspiration from Washington

The Department of Health and Human Services wanted to do good. Specifically, its Office of Inspector General (OIG)—which investigates Medicare fraud—wanted to do good. Beginning in 1994, with government shutdowns looming, the OIG was debating new ways to return more funds to the Medicare Trust Fund (which is another way of saying, your money and our money).

Inspiration struck when this government crew researched what other government agencies were up to—and saw that the FBI and the Drug Enforcement Agency (DEA) had teamed up on highly successful drug task forces involving organized crime.

The borrowed solution: Combine resources of the Medicare fraud trackers with teams from Health Care Financing Administration (HCFA) and the Administration on Aging to probe fraud in the home health industry and elsewhere.

Result: The Department invested $7 million of the people's Trust Fund in this operation and recovered $177 million in fines, restitutions, and savings.

Who says government can't turn a profit? It can if it can get beyond intramural bickering over turf.

Inspiration from Hilton Head

Jack McConnell, MD, retired from a rewarding career in medical research and bought a home in Hilton Head, South Carolina. It wasn't long before he decided there had to be more to retirement than honing his 16-handicap in golf. He looked around at Hilton Head's "other half" and saw the people who service the resorts and homes of those who can afford the good life. This other half work mostly for minimum wage and most can't afford even the basics of medical care.

Dr. McConnell went back to work. He networked with other retired doctors on the island, lobbied the town for resources, and soon opened the Volunteers in Medicine Clinic, fully staffed by retired doctors, nurses, and dentists. The clinic provides free medical care, head to toe, for people below a certain income level who are without medical coverage.

In year one, it had 5,000 patient visits. Years later, it had 16,000.

There are something like 150,000 retired doctors and 400,000 retired nurses in the United States, many of them itching to practice medicine and be productive again. At least 17 other free clinics have sprung up around the country, modeled on the Hilton Head success. Dozens more are in the works. Hundreds of other communities have contacted the good folks in Hilton Head for information.

Jack McConnell says his father, a Methodist preacher, used to come home every day and ask him and his six siblings: "And what did you do for someone today?"

Maybe today is your day to borrow a good idea at www .VIMclinic.org.

Borrowing for a Dinosaur

The Museum of Paleontology at the University of California at Berkeley held a dinosaur body-parts sale.

The museum asked contributors to sponsor parts of a *Tyrannosaurus rex* that had to be assembled. Donors' names would appear on a plaque at the museum. Prices ranged from $20 for a tailbone to $5,000 for the skull and jaws. (In case you're wondering, there are 300 pieces in your average T-Rex skeleton.)

The effort was a huge success. People bought parts in their kids' names. Grade schools held bake sales to sponsor a bone.

And where did this idea come from? It was borrowed. The body-parts fund drive was akin to an opera house or a synagogue having benefactors endow individual seats.

The Noninvitation Invitation

Lots of good causes could benefit from borrowing. Have you ever been invited to a big charity dinner that you really didn't want to attend? You just didn't want the hassle of getting a babysitter, renting a tuxedo, and sitting through all the speeches.

We understand, said some savvy folks in southern Florida. So they issued a "noninvitation" invitation for their event:

The annual Goodwill Industries dinner

will not be held this year at the Americana Hotel.

No cocktails will be served at 7 P.M.

No dinner will be served at 8 P.M.

The master of ceremonies will not be Art Linkletter.

The Rev. Norman Vincent Peale

will not read the invocation.

The guest speaker will not be Dear Abby.

Stay home and have a restful evening.

But please send $50 per person or $100 per couple.

Did this scheme work? Like gangbusters. It has since been adopted by other Goodwill chapters across the country.

Would it work for your favorite foundation?

Just ask Jack Evans, the CEO of Central Washington Hospital in Wenatchee, Washington. Jack heard us give this example during a management conference, went home and promptly stole the idea. Here is their noninvitation for the second annual Heart Center Campaign Dinner, part of a $500,000 fund-raising drive for the hospital's newly opened Cardiac Surgery Center:

Grace & Jim Lynch will again host our year-end event

at Central Washington Hospital.

Cocktails will *not* be hosted at 7 P.M.

Dinner will *not* be served at 8 P.M.

President Bill Clinton will *not* be our master of ceremonies.

The Rev. Billy Graham will *not* give the invocation.

Alan Greenspan, the Federal Reserve Chairman,

will *not* be our guest speaker.

Please join us—by staying at home and

having a restful evening.

But please send $50 per person or $100 per couple

to reach our campaign goal.

"It was the single most successful fund-raiser in our history," reports CEO Evans. (Their total costs for the "dinner" were a pittance for printing and postage.)

Would this idea work for your favorite foundation? Well, go ahead. Borrow it.

Borrow, Then Adapt

Long ago, in the September-October 1966 *Harvard Business Review*, Professor Ted Levitt observed: "In spite of the extraordinary outpouring of totally and partially new products and ways of doing things, by far the greatest flow of newness is not innovation at all. Rather, it is imitation."

The genius is in adapting someone else's solution to your problem. Maybe that idea will work unchanged and intact, "as is" for your purposes. More likely, you'll have to adapt it.

Think about FedEx and how it focuses on the single, primary vision that created the company in the first place: overnight delivery. FedEx has trained its workers to ship and track packages so efficiently that the U.S. Army, in designing the supply system for the Gulf War, applied the training techniques of FedEx.

Even the founder of FedEx, Fred Smith, had to borrow an idea when he was figuring out the most effective way to deliver overnight with a limited number of airplanes. He got the inspiration for pooling his planes in one place from the way banks pool their checks at a central clearinghouse.

The genius is in adapting someone else's solution to your problem. Maybe that idea will work unchanged and intact, "as is" for your purposes. More likely, you'll have to adapt it.

Fifty years ago, a gentleman named Alex Osborn set down a series of procedures for working with existing ideas to solve new problems.

Osborn was the "O" in the ad agency BBDO (Batten Barton Durstine & Osborn), and he spent a good portion of his life searching for more effective ways to generate good ideas. He called it "applied imagination." Among his procedures:

- Break problems into bite-size units that are easier to handle.
- Work on problem solving both individually and in group settings.
- Assume that most solutions will come from an association of ideas.
- Understand that existing ideas can be modified in dozens of different ways.

So we've taken the spirit of Thomas Edison's advice about adapting an existing idea to the problem you are currently working on. And we've adapted, expanded, and modernized Alex Osborn's methods for anyone searching for new ideas in 2002.

You're about to discover all the things you could do to elevate imitation to high art, and to make that borrowed idea your own.

CHAPTER

5

What Could You Substitute?

Panasonic replaced the normal cover of a notebook computer with a rugged shell and created its Tough-book line. Their hardy PCs could take a licking and keep on ticking.

A conference organization switched from expensive 4-color flyers to simple news releases to announce its new offerings to a mailing list of 5,000. Responses surged.

With a few changes in locale, era, and the names of characters (and with a little bit of help from Leonard Bernstein), Romeo and Juliet *became* West Side Story.

"To put or use a person or thing in place of another" is how the dictionary defines "Substitute."

What could you substitute in the approach, the materials, the ingredients or the appearance of what you've got? This technique is a proven winner when you're IdeaWise.

West Side Story is not an isolated example of substitution in the field of arts, where creativity is supposed to run rampant. A few years ago, the Hartford Ballet borrowed *The Nutcracker*, reset it in California in the 1800s, and added American Indians, Levi Strauss, and Mark Twain. The result: Boffo reviews for *The American Nutcracker*.

> *What could you substitute in the approach, the materials, the ingredients or the appearance of what you've got? This technique is a proven winner when you're IdeaWise.*

On May 8, 2001, a headline in *USA Today* read, "MTV modernizes masterpiece opera." Yes, MTV dragged opera kicking and screaming into the new century with *Hip-Hopera*. It's a retelling of *Carmen*, which was composed more than 125 years ago. Well, roll over Bizet, and tell Puccini the news.

If the creative community can win kudos with substituting, why not you and your company?

This Instead of That

Look no further than your desk. You're surrounded with success stories of companies that have substituted:

- That new Grip stapler made by Boston. It stands up. Instead of the ages-old stapler design that just sits there, this one stands upright. It's easier to grab and use in one motion.

- That Post-it notes dispenser. The original design is a pad that gets lost in the paper clutter. Once you find it, you have to move it into a writing position, then pull off the little yellow stickie. Instead, the new design has the note pop up and wave at you. It's ready for action.

- That cordless phone. Instead of a tangled cord, there's a hidden nickel cadmium battery. Carry it around and yak away to your heart's content without risk of strangulation.

The secret sauce of substitution is a little of "this" instead of some of "that." So, how should you proceed?

Easy. Just consider these possible avenues of exploration.

---

1. Substitute an ingredient.
2. Substitute a brand name.
3. Substitute automation.
4. Substitute manual labor.
5. Substitute to save.
6. Substitute in appearance.
7. Substitute someone else.

Now you're ready to put one thing in place of something else.

Substituting an Ingredient

The long history of inventions and innovations provides countless examples of how switching one ingredient or material or process opened up doors. That's how super-sweet Sugar Pops begat Corn Pops, a more nutrition-conscious cereal.

The state of Maryland asked itself, *"What could we substitute for tobacco?"* For 400 years, tobacco was a dependable and profitable crop, the foundation of the state's agricultural economy, the lifeblood of thousands of hard-working farmers on tens of thousands of rural acres. But tradition aside, is this a business you'd want your kids to inherit—with the avalanche of social, health, and economic sins now attached to smoking?

Those farms could grow other crops, reasoned the state. And part of a $5.5 billion national trust fund, reached through legal settlements with the tobacco companies, could be directed to help in that transition.

More than 75 percent of the state's tobacco farmers have said "yes" to the buyout program. In accepting the payments, they agree to refocus on other crops and to never again participate in the production of tobacco in Maryland. "Helping farmers transition from tobacco into life-sustaining crops is an essential part of our commitment to make Maryland a national leader in the battle against smoking, addiction, and tobacco-related diseases," said Governor Parris Glendening.

Ask yourself: If I replace an ingredient, can I do more and sell more?

- Changing components has given us remarkably improved electric lightbulbs. Decades before Thomas Edison came along, a scientist named De la Rue enclosed a platinum coil in a tube and passed an electric current through it. (His design worked, but the cost of this precious metal made his invention wildly impractical.) Later came charcoal filaments, carbonized fiber, Edison's first carbon filament that burned for only 40 hours, and tungsten filaments from GE. More recently, Philips substituted magnetic induction to excite a gas to emit light. (There are no parts to wear out and bulbs can last 60,000 hours.)

Ask yourself: If I replace an ingredient, can I do more and sell more?

- Just after World War I, DeWitt Wallace dreamed up the idea of a little magazine that would condense important articles. He called his modest notion *Reader's Digest,* which now sells 13 million copies monthly in the United States alone. With dozens of foreign editions, it's the most widely read magazine in the cosmos. Many decades later, a West Coaster named Dean Anderson asked himself, "What if I were to substitute and condense different kinds of articles?" His focus was the burgeoning health care field. Now each month, his company COR Healthcare Resources scans thousands of articles in hundreds of publications to produce a dozen successful newsletters for health care professionals. Titles range from *Clinical Excellence* to *Healthcare Market Strategist.*
- In the late 1970s, a Connecticut lawyer, Edward Packard, created a different kind of storybook to read to his kids. *The Cave of Time* was his first book, and it became the

first of a series of "Choose Your Own Adventure" books. A simple substitution, really: The books put readers in the driver's seat. As the readers reach numerous forks in the road of the plot, they decide which path to take, and then accept the consequences. ("The adventures you take are a result of your choice," it says on page one of Book One. "You are responsible because you choose.") The books were a huge hit with self-reliant kids who wanted to control things (and had a short attention span). Oh yes, at last count, more than 180 "Choose Your Own Adventure" titles have been published, with hundreds of million of copies in print.

- There's an activist consumer group that blames milk for everything from early-onset puberty to allergies to cancer. They champion pasteurized, refrigerated soy milk, which is low-fat, low-cholesterol, bovine-hormone free, full of protein, and tastes like milk (well, sort of). The leading brand, Silk, plays a multiple substitution game: It's soy milk instead of cow milk, and it's packaged in milk-like cartons. Can you call it milk if it doesn't come from a cow? ("Got soy?") Well, you can definitely call it profitable, at more than double the cost of cow milk.

- They're the size of a breath mint and they taste like one. But they pack a wallop because they're chock full of nicotine. It's a product called Ariva, intended for smokers at work, on airplanes, and in other situations where they can't light up. This cigarette substitute lozenge is made from powdered tobacco mixed with eucalyptus and mint flavoring.

Substituting a Brand Name

In the life of a business traveler, there are three constants:

1. Your flight will be delayed.
2. At journey's end, your hotel room will be at the end of a 1,500-kilometer labyrinth.
3. The food in the hotel's restaurant will be—well, better not to ask.

Hotel food has always had a suspect reputation. Nevertheless, every traveler expects that restaurant to be up and running. It's a meeting place for breakfast, lunch, and dinner. It's room service at odd hours.

What to do? If you're a luxury hotel, you might unburden yourself of running your own restaurant, substitute a big-name chef and a signature restaurant, and in the process connect with a global crowd. That happened when the tony Grand Bay Hotel in Coconut Grove, Florida, added a trendy eatery named Bice. Founded in Milan, Italy, Bice has branches in New York, Chicago, and Palm Beach.

What about a humbler midrange hotel chain targeted to the business traveler? The business crowd wants overall value, consistent quality, fast-paced dining options, and casual comfort without stuffiness.

Doubletree Club Hotels answered that tall order.

In place of a traditional hotel eatery, Doubletree substituted a partnership with the café-bakery chain Au Bon Pain. Just off the lobby, their hotels house a "Club Room," which is equal parts office, den, and café. It has work phones, computer hookups, and "Personal Harbor" work spaces by Steelcase (another recognizable brand name).

Center stage is a self-contained Au Bon Pain, which serves fresh, healthy food, including hot entrées, right in the Club Room. Or they'll deliver it to a meeting room or your hotel room.

Doubletree calls this, immodestly, a "business travel revolution."

Question: Is there some irksome part of your operation you could replace with a brand-name substitution?

Question: *Is there some irksome part of your operation you could replace with a brand-name substitution?*

Substituting Automation

- The first sewing machines were pedal-driven. Then electric motors took the place of foot power.
- Originally, windshield wipers and windows on cars were hand-cranked. Then came electric motors.

In Watsonville, California, the Granite Rock Company was selling rock and sand to local contractors. Renting trucks to move large quantities of construction material can cost a dollar or more a minute, so time was important.

What would speed things up? The company developed an automated loading system similar to a bank ATM machine. It accepted an identification card, released the materials, and printed a receipt. They called it the GraniteXpress system. Loading time used to be 24 minutes. Now customers could rock and roll in only seven minutes.

If you value your customers' time as much as their money, you might want to look into automating a straightforward transaction. Substituting speedy machinery for clerks can make a real difference. It can also free up your people for more scintillating work. It's no coincidence that Granite Rock has been named to *Fortune* magazine's "100 Best Places to Work" list for four consecutive years.

Substituting Manual Labor

But automation and technology aren't always the answer.

Sometimes, the simple screwdriver (99¢) is more valuable than the Multi-Head TwistoDriver XLT ($29.95, plus shipping).

Consider this urban drama played out every hour of every day. Paramedics perform lifesaving miracles in the darnedest places: On a roof, along train tracks, on an icy pond. There are no textbook calls for paramedics. Ever wonder what happens when they can't steer their big expensive rig through a crowd or a parade, or when there's really difficult terrain?

The director of one hospital's mobile intensive care unit described the scene he surveyed when asked to oversee emergency medical services at a summer festival. He said it was all spread out with a lake on one side and a guardrail that protected the lawn. It was a big field with road closures and no clear pathway. The only way he could imagine paramedics getting to someone, he realized, was on bikes.

That's right, bikes. Mountain bikes to be specific, which paramedics (and cops, and others) are substituting nationwide as the transportation of choice in tricky situations.

Think about the logistics of your business for a minute. Are you moving supplies or people in the most efficient way? What could you substitute?

Think about the logistics of your business for a minute. Are you moving supplies or people in the most efficient way? What could you substitute?

Substituting to Save

The boss is screaming bloody murder. Your department's meeting costs are through the roof. And you're not alone. As revenues weaken, many firms opt to trim back on travel. When the Big Dip of 2001 hit, travel consultants Runzheimer International said corporate travel budgets were slashed an average of 25 percent, and up to 50 percent in some cases.

Even so, your far-flung virtual team at Octopus Industries still needs some eyeball-to-eyeball time. What to do? Let's apply the principle of substitution to your budgeting dilemma:

- Instead of paying soaring air fares, you could substitute more teleconferences, videoconferences, and web conferences. The pictures and sound with services such as PictureTel are much improved. Sprint says its teleconferencing business jumped 10 percent in a single quarter of 2001.

- Instead of expensive hotels, you could switch to lower-priced spreads. Firms in New York, Chicago, Los Angeles, and other locales with ultraexpensive big-city hotels now are holding meetings in the suburbs.

- Instead of hotels and conference centers, you could use your own meeting space. To save money, Hewlett-Packard moved its annual summer meeting for security analysts from New York to a 150-seat auditorium at its Palo Alto headquarters. (For technology analysts who can't travel, the company broadcasts the session and Q&A period over the Internet.)

Maybe your financial squeeze demands more than slicing travel budgets. Maybe your company is facing layoffs.

Yes, there are creative ways of substituting even in the face of downsizing:

- *Consolidating offices.* Ad agencies or other service firms often find they can slash real estate costs by merging branches.

- *Sharing employees.* Some firms that have workers but not enough work are sharing their hires with other companies in need of staff.

- *Stock options instead of pay.* A database management firm in Arkansas mandated a pay cut of 5% in exchange for stock options. They also offered more options to workers who voluntarily took a bigger pay cut. (A third of their employees said yes.)

Substituting in Appearance

Down in the Big Easy (or Nawlins, as the locals say), the good times roll. But down at the Contemporary Arts Center on Camp Street in New Orleans, home to bold experimentations by campy artists, one solution didn't roll out so easily.

Their gallery space houses new works in painting, photography, music, video, sculpture, and performance art—none of which calls to mind the word "traditional." But what is traditional at this arts center, as in museums and galleries everywhere, is thanking the kind folks who fork over the money to make such artistic endeavors possible.

We're talking donors here. And like many other cultural institutions, the Center had planned a "donor wall" to acknowledge everyone by name.

Local companies, mostly sizable ones, provided big bucks. Above the company names, their logos were proudly displayed on a wall of stainless steel plaques. (Hey, we're talking contemporary art here. What were you expecting, mahogany?)

The vexing issue was what to do with all the individual donors who provided equally big bucks. The name of Mr. and Mrs. Horace Thibadeaux, stamped onto a plaque all by itself, just—well, it just sort of sat there. There would be no consistency of the artistic impression if names alone were to be stainlessly commingled with names with logos. What to do?

- Then, substitution inspiration struck the Contemporary Arts Center. What is a logo, after all, other than a unique graphic representation of a business? What is a unique graphic representation of a human donor—a fingerprint!

Yes, yes. We shall graft the actual thumbprints of Mr. and Mrs. Thibadeaux above their name, thus creating human logos!

Think about your company's appearance. Is it time for a substitution to upgrade a droopy color, a fussy typeface, or the wrong look?

- In the mid-1980s, Colgate-Palmolive purchased a Hong Kong company and inherited one of the best-selling toothpastes in several Asian countries. Its market share topped 50 percent in some of those lands. So far, so good. Except that the toothpaste was named Darkie and its package carried the unmistakable image of a minstrel in blackface.

Hark to some history: The minstrel became part of the design in the 1920s when the company's then-CEO saw American singer Al Jolson and thought his wide, white, toothy smile would make a swell logo. Move forward 60 years, and suddenly, Colgate had shareholder petitions demanding changes, religious groups decrying their motives, even an outraged U.S. Congressman joining the fracas.

Think about your company's appearance.
Is it time for a substitution to upgrade a droopy
color, a fussy typeface, or the wrong look?

What's a savvy CEO to do? Substitute for those damning identifiers, of course. Ruben Mark, chairman of the board at

Colgate-Palmolive, promptly announced that the toothpaste would be renamed Darlie (the substitution of just one letter made all the difference), and the logo would become a portrait of a man of ambiguous race wearing a silk top hat, tuxedo, and bow tie. Said the chairman: "It's just plain wrong. It's just offensive. The morally right thing dictated that we must change."

Colgate's change was shrewd. A drastically new name and totally different package would have wiped out the entire verbal and visual identity that was well-recognized by customers in Hong Kong, Malaysia, Singapore, Taiwan, and Thailand. Instead, the company substituted for the offensive features.

Sometimes, a substitution in appearance is more symbolic than practical:

- Toshiba Corporation is a sprawling high-tech Goliath that manufactures everything from washing machines to nuclear power plants to laptops. Its new president was determined to send a signal about where the company is headed. So he ordered the dismantling of a fast-breeder reactor model that had greeted employees and visitors for 15 years in the company's Tokyo headquarters. The planned substitution: futuristic Toshiba televisions or e-commerce kiosks.

Substituting Someone Else

Premio Foods makes the tastiest Italian sausage in the United States. Decades ago, grandfather handed down the hearty recipes from his home in Italy. The company buys specially selected cuts of pork from exclusive suppliers and grinds them immediately with a secret blend of fresh spices to produce tantalizing aroma and robust flavor.

If you're the marketing *padrone* at Premio, you already know the taste buds on the right side of the consumer's food brain will jump up and say, *"Stupendo!"* But the rational left side of the brain has no such evidence. You can't "prove" that taste claim in any objective way.

But you could. You could prove it in the way that others have demonstrated their preference:

- Lexus built its business around J.D. Powers surveys on customer satisfaction ratings.
- Schwab touts its online brokerage services by pointing to its overall top ratings in *Money, Smart Money,* and *PC World* magazines.
- "Nine out of ten screen stars," proclaimed a 1927 ad, "care for their skin with Lux toilet soap."

Hmmm. Time for a bit of the old *this-for-that.* On behalf of your zesty sausage, what could you substitute in place of one of those polls, panels, or expert reports? Let's go in search of authenticity:

- You could conduct your own study. Hire a research company to do blind taste tests outside supermarkets. (And hey, if you don't win, nobody ever has to know!)
- Or, cozy up to a food editor. Suggest a newspaper or magazine conduct their own taste preference research. Food

writers do this all the time, for everything from wine to mail-order steaks.

- Or, offer to supply the Italian sausage at one of the major Italian-American festivals. Then, proclaim yourself "The Official Italian Sausage of . . ."

Heed this counsel from Stanley Resor, a founder of J. Walter Thompson.

"We want to copy those whom we deem superior in taste or knowledge or experience."

In other words, substitute someone else.

CHAPTER

6

What Could You Combine?

Team-building.

That's the current clarion call of some management theorists.

"Build a team. Craft a team. Mold a team," they say, and innovative solutions will flow to the firm and rising profits will flow to the income statement. Individuals, says this wisdom, can't move organizations by themselves. Neither can a few superstars. Rather, it takes a team (or a "village" if you're Hillary Clinton).

But does it? Not really.

Oh sure, teams of employees pulling together, like the oarsmen in a crew, can be most successful. And at times, for certain organizations in certain situations, team building makes real sense. But let's face it, people forced to work together in a team can also turn out to be real pains in the tush. Pushy. Picky. Argumentative. Obnoxious. Even downright nasty.

So team building isn't always the panacea the management consultants would have you believe. Building a team can be fraught with risk. Not only are individual workers crunched together in a jury-rigged aggregation no guarantee for success, they can be counterproductive to an organization trying to build innovation, entrepreneurship, and esprit.

But whereas forcing employees to work on teams may not yield the desired results, combining one or two individuals or ideas or products or processes can lead to organizational breakthroughs.

Think about it.

Combining Abbott with Costello, Mork with Mindy, Bialystock with Bloom, Laverne with Shirley, Lennon with McCartney, peanut butter with jelly, fish with chips, arroz con pollo, Rivkin with Seitel (well, okay, at least arroz con pollo).

"An idea grows," somebody once observed, "by annexing its neighbors."

In each case, the combination clinched the deal and made the sum far greater than the parts.

"Combining," the dictionary says, "is the act of uniting to achieve a socal, political, or economic end."

"An idea grows," somebody once observed, "by annexing its neighbors."

When you're IdeaWise, strategic combinations can lead to breakthrough ideas that mark real progress and earn fat profits.

The Laker Tree

Combinations that click often lead to additional combinations that also click. "Contagious combination clicking" is what you might call it. We would call it *the Laker Tree:*

- For many years throughout the 1980s, the Los Angeles Lakers were the NBA's *Showtime.* Three individuals ruled the LA roost. Dapper Pat Riley coached. Magical "Magic" Johnson set the table. And omnipresent Kareem Abdul-Jabbar nailed down the victories. The rest of the team was a mixture of interchangeable parts that played solidly, if not spectacularly, in clearly subordinate roles. It was because of the three-man combo that the Lakers dominated the league.

And then, as do all good things, the Laker dynasty came to an end. Riley left for New York. Kareem departed for the movies. And Magic became a businessman. In their place arrived names like Benoit Benjamin, Sedale Threatt, and Randy Pfund. They were all nice people, good and decent men, who got along well and worked together as a team. But the results weren't exactly "pfabulous."

The team was mired in mediocrity.

In fact, it wasn't until the Lakers recruited three other unique individuals and meshed them in a new combination that the team's fortunes turned around.

Shaquille O'Neal was the grand intimidator. But he couldn't win until the Lakers recruited Kobe Bryant, the teenage prodigy. And for three maddening years, even these two superstars could not lead the team to an NBA championship, until they were combined with Phil Jackson, the coaching Zen master.

Three big men. Three big egos. Three individuals. In combination.

And the new three-man combo, once again surrounded by role players, hasn't looked back since.

And what about the *Laker Tree?* Well, consider all the other combinations that have sprouted from the budding Laker dynasty:

- Staples, the office supply giant, yearned to be associated with the victorious Laker juggernaut and so sponsored the construction of a new house of worship for the Shaq-Jack-Kobe trio, and named the new roundball shrine for itself. The Staples Center has now successfully combined corporate Staples with the Laker success.

- Basketball shoe giant Adidas, playing second fiddle to arch-enemies Nike and Reebok, snagged young Kobe as its corporate mouthpiece and converted him into a philosopher prince. On Adidas commercials, Kobe spoke inspiringly of the spirit of "innovation" and "invention." And the Adidas-Bryant combination led Kobe wannabes of every stripe to dream of the potential of their own hardcourt creativity, merely by lacing on a pair of sneakers. Adidas sales soared.

- Candy maker Nestlé, mired with an anachronistic crunch bar in an era of Gobstoppers, Gummi Bears, and chocolate Twizzlers, latched onto the King Court Cruncher himself, and the combination of Nestlés Crunch and chief spokesperson Shaq helped revive the venerable candy brand.

- And finally, the Laker Girls, also inextricably intertwined with the success of the dominant threesome on the court, gradually replaced their counterparts from the Dallas Cowboys, as the most coveted cheerleaders in the nation for calendars, cover stories, and personal appearances.

The *Laker Tree* is a powerful concept for any organization; testimony to the value of winning combinations that expand and nourish each other. Such combinations rise above the din of mediocrity, breathe new life into old ideas, and reinvigorate the people and the products on which organizations depend.

The Power of Combinations

First there was plain old yogurt, a product so bland it had to be combined with vanilla (vanilla!) to give it some personality. But then, the yogurt industry got busy:

- Vanilla was combined with flavors such as strawberry, banana, and chocolate.

- Flavored yogurt was combined with real fruit—cherries, peaches, and apples.
- Fruit yogurt was combined with nuts.
- Fruit and nut yogurt was combined with granola.
- Fruit-nut-granola yogurt was combined with sprinkles and toppings.

And the yogurt industry reinvigorated itself, all due to combinations.

To use the power of combinations to introduce new ideas, you don't have to be yogurt or flavored or even nuts to escape the plain vanilla of your industry, product mix, organizational structure, or personnel alignment.

Paul Simon was asked where he got the inspiration for "Bridge over Troubled Water." He said he was carrying around two melodies in his head—a Bach chorale and a gospel tune from the Swan Silvertones—"and I just pieced them together," . . . into one of the biggest smash hits in the history of modern music.

> *To use the power of combinations to introduce new ideas, you don't have to be yogurt or flavored or even nuts to escape the plain vanilla of your industry product mix, organizational structure, or personnel alignment.*

So, too, can you piece together the things that surround you to further your product line, your organization, and yourself. It's that simple.

The Art of the Combo

In the typical twenty-first-century nuclear family habitat, you eat alone much of the time. With the kids at the ball field and the wife at her second job, it is left to the lord of the manor to prepare the dinner feast.

In such a situation, your thoughts may turn to salad. But if all you have is lettuce and tomato, the salad ain't hardly worth it. So you chop up some of those baby carrots, and you throw in a few olives, toss in some mushrooms. And grab some of that cheese block that's been sitting in the fridge and, while you're at it, a couple of pressed turkey slices, too. And how about pieces of that orange to spice things up. And there's a jar of bacon bits and a hard-boiled egg and jicama (jicama?). Whatever, throw it in there. Top off with croutons and grated Parmesan, and douse generously with Golden Honey Dijon Marinade dressing.

And voilà! You have used combinations to create a masterpiece (not to mention further the fortunes of the folks who make Pepto-Bismol).

The same thing happens with creativity. An idea is picked up from one place, attached to an idea from another place, and the combination yields something brand-spanking new.

Many regard *synthesis*, the act of combining elements, as the essence of creativity. Just as substituting one thing for another can yield something original, so, too, can combining properties.

Combinations can create healthy profits, too. In the supermarket, orange juice enhanced with calcium was just the start.

Sales of foods with added vitamins and minerals are a $17 billion business, growing twice as fast as other food categories, according to Nutrition Business International.

An idea is picked up from one place, attached to an idea from another place, and the combination yields something brand-spanking new.

Best of all, coming up with winning combinations doesn't require seeking out an idea guru in the mountains of Nepal. The technique is simple. Conceiving creative combinations begins, curiously enough, by *separating* the exercise into bite-sized avenues of exploration, such as:

1. Combine individual ingredients, multiple components, or materials.
2. Combine whole products or services.
3. Combine product uses.
4. Combine organizational functions.
5. Combine organizations themselves.
6. Combine with the World Wide Web.

Combining the Components

"What materials can we combine?"

Every product or service is made up of specific components. By deconstructing the product and separating it into its component parts, a new product, with different attributes and appeals, might be created.

Coming up with combinations requires an operating premise that states a real business challenge and solves it by combining ingredients. For example, ever since Clarence Birdseye developed the quick-freezing process in the 1920s, food manufacturers have rushed to create convenience products. Today, when increasing numbers of people are too busy even to eat an apple or peel an orange, the need for ultraconvenience products has accelerated. So food makers combine things:

- Iced tea.

Operating premise: No time to boil water, and then cool it.
Combination solution: Lipton sells a tea bag that lets you brew iced tea in cold water, thus saving the time and sparing the patience it would have taken to make tea using boiling water and then cooling it down.

- Toothpaste.

Operating premise: No time to use both toothpaste and mouthwash.
Combination solution: Colgate introduces a "2-in-1" product that combines the two breath savers. Listerine goes it one better by introducing its own toothpaste, hinting at the same combination from the world's most revered brand of mouthwash.

- Cereal.

Operating premise: No time to wolf down breakfast.
Combination solution: Take the milk, add the cereal, and combine them both in a bar that people can take on the bus, in

the car, to the train. General Mills Milk 'n Cereal bars, with Cheerios on the outside and a creamy, real milk filling on the inside, negate the need for bowl, spoon, or time.

Combining existing ingredients or elements or materials to create something new and unique and groundbreaking works in any industry. Just as you "dance with the girl who brung you to the party," so, too, should you create with the components on which the organization depends:

- Television.

Operating premise: The unwritten rule of TV creativity is "pushing the envelope," constantly introducing ever more edgy fare—confrontational talk shows, reality programming, controversial sitcoms, hardcore dramas.

Combination solution: Use the tried-and-true elements of traditional television to create something new.

Behold Ken Burns.

The documentary producer extraordinaire has put together multipart series for Public Broadcasting on subjects as arcane as baseball, jazz, and the Civil War. His documentaries are a series of combinations of the oldest elements in the TV book—still photos, old footage, transitional music, and talking head interviews. But when Burns combines these ingredients, he produces an enchanting elixir that becomes not only riveting television but also something brand-new.

- And speaking of "elixirs," if you're a maker of the finer spirits, how in the world do you muscle your way to recognition, with the competition increasing by the minute?

Take vodka. You've got old standbys like Smirnoff and Stoli and new bar favorites, like Ketel One and Grey Goose. Compounding the choices, you've got cheap vodkas, expensive vodkas, Russian vodkas, multidistilled vodkas, and on and on.

So what does Absolut vodka do to differentiate itself from all these alternative providers? It seeks out combinations of ingredients to spice up its nectar—citron, mandarin orange, pepper, vanilla, and raspberry. Raspberry vodka?

Absolut-ly.

And the success of Absolut's flavored line has forced competitors to defend their turf by introducing combinations of their own. Such is the power of creativity through combining components.

Combining Whole Products

"What products can we combine?"

Most organizations have a roster of product or service offerings that exist in isolation, with their own product managers, marketing teams, advertising programs, and P&L reporting lines. By combining whole products or services—and, if necessary, breaking the bonds of organizational structural straitjackets—brand-new customer offerings can sometimes be created.

This is the mix-and-match premise that most of us engage in every morning. "I'll wear this blue shirt and my power red tie. No, doggone it, I'm gonna get crazy and pick this yellow paisley tie and see what happens." Or, "I'll try this brown skirt with this mauve blouse," if you're a working woman (or a more daring man).

The point is that "variety" is the spice of life, and product combinations are the source of product line variety:

- In the noncarbonated beverage industry, they've already "milked" (sorry) all the ingredients they can into teas and juices—strawberry tea, blueberry tea, cinnamon tea, apple-cranberry juice, banana-berry juice, and so on. New ingredients have all dried up (sorry again).

So what do you do now to extend the product portfolio even further?

You combine the beverages themselves. This is exactly what PepsiCo has done by combining tea with juice and creating a brand-new drink it calls Matika. With names like Skyhigh Berry, Dragonfruit Potion, and Mythical Mango, each drink combines 5 percent juice with black or green tea, cane sugar, and ginseng. From existing products, a new category of beverage, with potential for new profitability, has been created.

- This is the same rationale that drove (again, so sorry) General Motors to combine its SUV and its pickup truck into the new, mammoth SUV-pickup combination, the Chevrolet Avalanche. GM wants to shake its stodgy image as a purveyor of dependable but dull automobiles. The imaginative route it has chosen to shake the cobwebs is through combinations.

The Avalanche joins another combination crossover vehicle in the GM stable, the Buick Rendezvous, which combines a minivan with a sport utility sedan. If your organization is conservative, turning to product combinations is a relatively safe way to demonstrate creativity.

That is not to say that the most creative organizations don't also seek out combinations to rejuvenate profitability:

- Few companies are more imaginative than Walt Disney Company. But when Disney's California Adventure theme park in Anaheim got off to sluggish sales in 2001, the company turned to combinations to jump-start attendance. It introduced a new ticketing policy that allowed California Adventure customers immediate entry to its neighboring Disneyland theme park as well. By combining access to the two parks with one admission ticket, the company created a new inducement for visitors and a new opportunity for revenue for itself.

If your organization is conservative, turning to product combinations is a relatively safe way to demonstrate creativity.

The dilemma for any mature product—whether Disneyland, tea, or SUV—is how to breathe new life into something that has become tired, mundane and commonplace. One foolproof option is to inventory pooped-out products and rejuvenate them through a combination with another product:

- The HJ Heinz company has, for years, produced the world's most venerable ketchup and barbecue sauces. And its challenge is to reinvigorate its sauces to keep attracting new users.

So what did Heinz do to "spice up" the sauce? It combined it with, well, "sauce"—liquor, that is. In 2001, Heinz teamed with Brown-Forman's Jack Daniel's whiskey product to introduce three new barbecue sauces offering the famous Tennessee whiskey taste.

And not to worry that little Leroy will start to stagger after smothering his burger with the new recipe. The new flavors are nonalcoholic, as all alcohol is cooked off in manufacture, leaving behind only the rich essence of Jack Daniel's.

And if combining barbecue sauce with liquor or vodka with raspberries doesn't seem, at first blush, to make sense to you, blush again. The art of combining two dissimilar products to create a brand-new one is another high-potential avenue toward successful innovation.

Combining the Uses

"What product uses can we combine?"

Let's say you just arrived in town, it's late, and you're thirsty from the long flight. You stop to pick up a bottle of soda before checking in at the hotel. But once you get up to the room, sure enough, there's no bottle opener.

So what do you do? Of course, you improvise by cleverly using the latch designed to lock the door as a substitute bottle opener. After jamming the bottle cap down on the latch and carefully brushing away the glass shards—you've got a refreshing beverage.

Similarly (or perhaps not exactly similarly), just because your organization's products or services were designed to perform a certain function doesn't mean they can't be used for something else. Combining product uses to save time is another route to innovation, whether we're talking basketballs or toilet tissues:

- Anybody who has ever laced 'em up to shoot some hoops in the driveway knows the frustration of discovering nothing in the garage but sagging basketballs. Finding those elusive needles to inflate the ball is like, well, searching through a haystack.

The Spalding sporting goods company has found the answer—combine the needle with the ball. Spalding's Infusion basketball has a built-in pump technology, so you can blow it up and then play in one easy motion.

- In a completely different area, the Kimberly-Clark Corporation, makers of dry toilet tissue for adults and moist towelettes for babies, has come up with something completely different in an area that has remained the same for a century, toilet paper.

Since one of four adults use a moist tissue after going to the bathroom, Kimberly Clark has introduced Cottonelle Fresh Rollwipes, which hang from a dispenser above a family's dry toilet paper and are flushable. The company is betting—close to $200 million to manufacture and market the adult wet wipes—that by offering products that combine the activities of relieving oneself and then washing, it can broaden its leadership in the $800 million U.S. moist towelette market.

Old-line companies, in particular, producers of traditional products that today are being challenged by new technology, would be wise to combine product uses to rejuvenate their lines:

- One such venerable organization that has hit on harder times is Rochester's Eastman Kodak, photographic supplier since time began but now being challenged by Fuji and others. Today, Kodak has hooked up with Boston's new wave LifeFX to combine photo imaging with e-mail. The resultant Facemail combines images with words to deliver personalized Web picture greetings, with audio soon to be added.

Old-line companies, in particular, producers of traditional products that today are being challenged by new technology, would be wise to combine product uses to rejuvenate their lines.

Coming up with combined uses needn't be so technical. Nor do use combinations need be directed at products and services:

- Bank branches open up their lobbies for use as after-hours community meeting sites.
- Management consultants distribute their in-house magazines externally to clients and prospects for use as public relations tools.

- Even the Zamboni machine that methodically smooths the ice surface during hockey intermissions doubles as an advertising vehicle.

The art of combining uses of products, services, or even facilities is another way to breathe innovative life into an organization.

Combining Organizational Functions

"What organizational units or functions can we combine?"

The organization that doesn't continually question why it does things the way it does is likely to get "Xeroxed" with a capital "X." Once the epitome of a well-managed, smoothly run company, Xerox Corporation got too tied to its old ways and now struggles for survival.

"Because we've always done it this way" is no longer sufficient to explain why the organization operates in a certain manner. Just as products and services can be combined to create innovations, so, too, can organizational functions be brought together to yield new efficiencies and even enhanced client service.

The classic example brings together product and service functions under one umbrella. This approach is increasingly popular among the heaviest of heavy equipment manufacturers:

- General Electric's jet engine business, as gritty an industrial operation as you'll find, sells an airline a guaranteed level of engine uptime for the contracted period.

How can it make such a bold guarantee? It combines with the sale, such backup functions as parts, repairs, replacement engines, even financing—whatever it takes to make the plane fly.

- GE competitor Alstom USA, maker of all matter of boilers and turbines, dedicates internal alliances, combinations of various relationship and service departments, to ensure that individual client account needs get met with minimum delay and bureaucracy.

The less classic example, in this day of dwindling resources, is to bring together organizationally, functions that regularly work together. This can either be done by combining internal functions, or even bringing in-house some outsourced functions:

- At Boston Medical Center, the hospital that provides medical care for more poor people than any other facility in Massachusetts, pediatricians got so tired of seeing malnourished and inadequately treated babies, they brought in their own lawyers to confront the problem. They moved a staff of three lawyers into the Pediatrics Department to deal directly with the legal and administrative battles that the doctors deemed necessary to improve children's health. In this way, the legal beagles were closer to the action and could respond more quickly to pressing problems.
- LifeCare Hospitals of Dallas, Texas, has come up with an innovative way to treat acutely ill patients. It combines all the medical disciplines required for a particular patient's

health care needs—orthopedics, oncology, physical therapy, psychology, and so on—into one team to deal collectively with improving wellness.

Similarly, many companies have brought together promotion-oriented functions such as advertising, marketing, merchandising, and public relations to form integrated marketing departments that coordinate cohesive promotional campaigns for the company's products and services.

Companies also have found it expeditious to bring outside functions, such as legal or advertising or public relations, in-house, either to cut costs or improve responsiveness, or both:

- JC Penney achieved this in two steps. First, it inventoried its extensive legal work, consolidated assignments through improved technology and paralegal staffing, and was able to trim headcount. Next, it inventoried all the work done by its 150 different law firms—ooofa!—and took the time to separate the work into several distinct categories. The effort was well worth it, as Penney was able to combine its external legal work among six preferred providers.

No organizational approach or function should be untouchable in this era of unrestrained competition and scarce resources. Everything should be questioned.

No organizational approach or function should be untouchable in this era of unrestrained competition and scarce resources. Everything should be questioned. Combining organizational functions for better overall results is one viable answer.

Combining Organizations

"What organizations can we combine?"

To many, the word "merger" is as welcome as the cry of "food fight." Mergers often mean downsizing, ill will, and new internal animosities that take years to mend:

- White shoe lawyers Clifford Chance of England and Rogers & Wells of New York merge as one and almost rip out each other's throats, backing opposing clients in an intellectual property dispute.
- Long-time Wall Street rivals Chase Manhattan and J.P. Morgan merge to form J.P. Morgan Chase. But the new name fits a lot better than the new affiliation, which is marked by sharp elbows and backbiting throughout the ranks.

Mergers of entire organizations should be approached with great caution. Sometimes the same is true of organizational affiliations (e.g., Ford Motor Company and Bridgestone/Firestone, Inc.).

But that's the bad news, and hey, we're good news guys and this is a good news book. So what you need to realize is that combining your operation with somebody else's aura may be all you need to jump-start the organization and its offerings.

On the profit-making side, alliances are forming in waves:

- Because of a successful alliance, Mercedes-Benz doesn't even build its own E Class cars. The Magna Corporation does the work, including final assembly.
- Nestlé USA candy makers have teamed with Bestfoods' Skippy Peanut Butter to take peanut butter and jelly to the next level. Peanut Butter with Nestlé Crunch is a natural. And Nestlé plus Skippy is a can't miss affiliation.
- Suburu has teamed with outdoor outfitter L.L. Bean to offer an L.L. Bean edition of what else?—its Outback station wagon.
- Dell, responding to the slump in PC sales, promotes its quality partners, Microsoft and Intel, by stamping their corporate logos on Dell computers.

On the nonprofit side, meanwhile, the same thing is happening:

- Harvard and Stanford, the collegiate crème de la crème on either coast but formerly bitter rivals, plan to merge part of their vaunted business school operations. The result will be a separate entity that will design and deliver face-to-face and online programs to companies around the world.
- Other universities including Duke, Alabama, and Arkansas have teamed up with the Alltel wireless company to create cell phones with school logos and colors. Alltel sales surged 30 percent.
- The Florida State Department of Citrus teamed with the A.M. Braswell, Jr. Food Company to develop a new line of

Citrus Creations Jam, featuring Florida's finest citrus fruits. The sales revenue sure beats raising the money through taxes.

Combining organizations also might mean creating networks that deliver your services through affiliates in different geographies. Networks make sense for any small and even not-so-small service provider:

- The Harmonie Group is a network of 60 litigation firms ranging in size from 12 lawyers to more than 200 lawyers who specialize in noncriminal defense. For smaller members, Harmonie offers referral business from far-off markets. For larger members, Harmonie offers not only referral targets but potential acquisitions.

Combining organizations also might mean creating networks that deliver your services through affiliates in different geographies.

Similar networks are common in the service fields of advertising, marketing, public relations, management consulting, e-branding, and many others.

The omnipresent combinations in airports, shopping malls, on Main Streets, and in movie theaters—Baskin-Robbins with Dunkin' Donuts, Taco Bell with Nathan's—don't just happen. Corporate thinkers cogitate on the pros and cons of such affiliations.

Often, the act of combining the prestige and products of one organization with those of another makes great sense.

Combining with the World Wide Web

"What do we have that could be combined with the Web?"

Behold the Internet: repository of all information, channel of easiest accessibility, destroyer of all personal investment wealth (at least recently).

Considering how you might combine products or services or activities on the Web ought to be an obligatory exercise for any new idea-conscious organization.

"Does the brand naturally extend to the Internet? Will we target the same or different segments on the Net? How will we price on the Net? What promotional scheme will we adapt to get you there, and what incentives will we offer once you arrive?" These are the kinds of questions you should ask about combining with the Web.

Internet combinations extend far and wide, from books and broadcasts to hammers and nails to malted milk ball gelato ice cream:

- Barnes & Noble didn't knuckle under when it was confronted by the most formidable retailer on the Web, Amazon.com. It met its new competition toe-to-toe with Barnesandnoble.com. And although neither bookseller is tearing up the track, in stock market terms, Barnes & Noble's Internet combination made great strategic sense in the retail marketplace.

- Office Depot goes one step further, tightly integrating its Web site and its physical stores to form a single, seamless retailing network. "The Internet is just another channel that gets plugged into the business architecture," is how

Office Depot executives explain the Officedepot.com combination.

- Ashton Technology, Philadelphia-based trading systems company, was faced with increasing the flow of stockholder information, by virtue of the SEC's Fair Disclosure Rule. It chose to meet the new requirement by having shareholders submit e-mail questions to the CEO and answering them through a monthly webcast.

The movies, too, have combined the Internet to innovate in a huge way:

- The granddaddy of all Web movie promotions was the historic *Blair Witch Project,* a little bitty horror flick that cost $35,000 to shoot and grossed $50 million in its first month. How? By promoting itself online.

The young filmmakers launched www.blairwitch.com a year before the film's debut. It was a thoroughly realistic-looking report of the mysterious disappearance of young filmmakers in the midst of filming a movie called the *Blair Witch Project.* It was art imitating art imitating art.

Blair Witch Project opened the gates to Web promotions as an imperative in selling feature films. It wasn't long before moviegoers were complaining that movie-tied Internet previews were more entertaining than the films they promoted.

That's exactly what happened with *A.I.,* Steven Spielberg's 2001 paean to computer-driven life forms. Spielberg started the buzz for the movie with an ambitious Internet game that attracted waves of publicity and a cult following of its own. Summarized one chat room denizen, "The game is great. The movie is garbage."

- American Express, which has introduced gold cards, platinum cards, and super platinum cards, merely had to embed a microchip in a plain old card to arrive at its potentially greatest innovation. The chip allows card holders to make secure online purchases via a special reader hooked up to a computer. Amex's new Blue credit card found its way into 1.5 million wallets in just 15 months.

- And if ice cream can be sold via the Net, any product can be. IceCreamSource.com guarantees its Web offerings will arrive frozen with a 100 percent satisfaction. If you're not pleased, you're not obligated. IceCreamSource.com markets nearly 20 brands and more than 200 flavors, including the always appropriate malted milk ball gelato.

Any organizational activity, any organizational function, any organizational department ought to be thinking of combining with the World Wide Web for beneficial innovation.

In such creative combinations, there is strength, hope, and potential payoff.

CHAPTER 7

What Could You Magnify or Minimize?

The bigger, the better—that's how we like it.

Fat one-pound cheeseburgers at Fuddrucker's with triple cheese. Super Big Gulps at 7–Eleven with 44 ounces of cascading refreshment. Humongous SUVs that crowd everything else off the road. Mid-American megamalls big enough to lose your momma. Gargantuan Las Vegas hotels with more sprawl than some cities. Big hair, big opportunity, big attitude. And then there's Texas.

As Mr. Austin Powers would say, "Yeahhhhh, baby!"

Wait, hold that thought. We could be wrong.

Less is more—that's how we like it.

Tiny cellphones that curl up in the palm of your hand. Pint-sized cameras that go anywhere. Lilliputian umbrellas that fit in purses and briefcases. Dainty travel sizes of shampoo and tooth-paste. Virtual companies with three employees and one computer. Researchers in nanomedicine with miniscule "smart bombs" that find cancer cells, kill them with lasers, and then report the kills. Life in small-town USA is the American dream.

As Austin Powers's alter ego, Dr. Evil, would say, "You're the greatest, Mini-Me."

Small is beautiful. Yeah, that's the ticket.

The Dichotomy

The truth is, we love 'em big *and* we love 'em small. That's the wonderful dichotomy of Americana circa 2002—our dual love affair with both extremes of the size and structure poles.

What about big lumbering dogs like Newfoundlands, tipping the scales at 140 pounds? They're very much in demand. Itsy-bitsy pooches like two-pound Yorkshire Terriers? Wildly popular.

What about megaresorts on Maui with a thousand rooms, ten swimming pools, and eight restaurants? Can't get a reservation in high season. Or a cozy bed and breakfast with four rooms on a winding country lane? Nope, nothing available until next year.

The larger truth be known, the United States has always had this bifurcated love affair. In the 1880s, John D. Rockefeller,

then the richest man on the planet, merged 40 allied companies to create the Standard Oil Trust, a sweeping monopoly
that controlled exploration, production, distribution, and
marketing. He was the "mine's-bigger-than-yours" Bill Gates
of his era.

---

*The larger truth be known, the United States
has always had this bifurcated love affair.*

On the other hand, speaking of Mr. Gates, now the richest
man on the planet, his technology pioneered the era of "the
smaller the better." Computers depend on tiny wafers and
chips to store millions of megabytes and gigabytes and any
other quantity of bites you can muster. Increasingly smaller (or
is that decreasingly smaller?) wireless, hand-held computers
and insulated chips—faster, more efficient, more compact—
promise to pace the next leg of the computer age.

In fact, all things considered, it's a grand time to be big, or
small. And when you book passage for an IdeaWise journey, it's
a grand time to think through all the possibilities.

---

1. Construct it bigger, or smaller.
2. Amplify or reduce the numbers.
3. Magnify or minimize the possibilities.
4. Make it last a longer or shorter time.
5. Expand or constrict your customer relationship.
6. Give it more—or less—sensory sensation.

Constructing It Bigger or Smaller

Humans tend to equate bigness with success, stature, and leadership. We give respect and admiration to the biggest.

In their book *Mindwatching: Why People Behave the Way They Do*, psychologists Hans and Michael Eysenck reported on a famous study of size. A man named "Mr. England" was introduced to classes of college students in the United States. He was referred to as either "Mr. England, a student from Cambridge" or as "Professor England from Cambridge." Afterward, the students were asked to estimate the man's height. As Mr. England climbed in status from student to professor, he gained five inches in the eyes of the students.

Professor England would be right at home at www .ThinkBig.com—the online home for 600 stores that specialize in fashions for big and tall guys. After he slips on his size 48XL Austin Reed navy blazer, our prototypical Big Guy might want to:

- Pick up a few Easter eggs for the kids' party. Maybe the seven-pound, 17-inch tall behemoth of chocolate Easter eggs from Lunettes et Chocolat ($200 the egg).
- Take his overgrown appetite over to the nearest Fuddrucker's for their giant one-pound hamburger (a mere $6.99).
- Slosh that down with a 44-ounce Super Big Gulp at 7–Eleven. No wait, now there's a 64-ounce Double Big Gulp . . . and over at Circle K there's the two-quart Ultimate Thirst Buster . . . and over at Unocal's Fast Break there's the 64-ounce Power Splash.

- Drive his land yacht—excuse us, his sports utility vehicle— along a 12-lane freeway where his hulking, four-ton, V-10 beast will basically blot out the sun.

- And complete his well-rounded journey with a visit to the Massachusetts Museum of Contemporary Art, probably the largest center for visual and performing arts in the world. (It took over an abandoned 13-acre factory complex and has galleries the size of football fields.)

That's what any big-thinking citizen could call a full day.

On the other hand, a funny thing happened on the path to populating the earth with all these megasize products. People and companies and industries began to see the value in "thinking small":

- The biotechnology industry discovered the microscopic science of genomics, and our bodies will never be the same again.

Based on the genetic structure of human cells, themselves ridiculously tiny and efficient, the study of genomics is well down the road to categorizing the genetic makeup of individual cells, isolating the three billion As, Cs, Gs, and Ts packed into a nucleus one hundredth of a millimeter across.

The sequencing of DNA in biotech undertakings like the Human Genome Project will revolutionize health care, science, and our knowledge of ourselves, as researchers unlock the tiniest particles that make us tick.

- Meanwhile, the technological equivalent of the human mind, the computer industry, continues to miniaturize.

Intel is experimenting with an elfin chip that will combine three computer processes in one: flash memory for data storage, microprocessor logic for computing functions, and analog circuits for communications. Such minimalist innovations are what the high-tech industry is counting on to resurrect it after the burst bubble at the turn of the new century.

- On the consumer side, look what's happened to those *Stegosaurus*-sized SUVs; they, too, have gotten smaller.

The real action in the SUV category is at the other end of the spectrum, in the so-called baby UTEs. Mid-sized and smaller SUVs—Ford's Escape, Toyota's RAV4, Subaru's Forester, and the rest—account for 60 percent of cardom's hottest market. They're cheaper, sportier, and consume less gas. Who knows? Maybe the United States will soon be ready for DaimlerChrysler's new Smart Car, which at 98.4 inches, is 40 percent smaller than the Volkswagen Beetle.

- In financial services, automated teller machines used to be those big, entrenched clunkers in bank lobbies. Today, they are sleek little cash kiosks in restaurants, supermarkets, and between the men's and women's restrooms (right where the cigarette machine used to be) in some of the nation's finest shops.

And in terms of whole companies and industries, it is the occasional peewee purveyor that leaves the big boys in their tracks.

- Lehman Brothers is the rare small player in the investment banking business. With a market cap of $19 billion, Lehman is positively puny compared to competitors Merrill Lynch and Morgan Stanley Dean Witter & Co., with market caps respectively of $50 and $71 billion.

But in 2001, as the Merrills and the Morgans and the Goldman Sachses posted declines and fired staff, Lehman recorded increased profits and added employees. An independent banker for 150 years, Lehman has demonstrated that staying small and targeted makes a lot more sense than bulking up and losing focus.

Think about constructing a bigger or smaller size of what your organization delivers; it makes irrefutable innovative sense.

Think about constructing a bigger or smaller
size of what your organization delivers; it
makes irrefutable innovative sense.

Amplifying or Reducing the Numbers

AMC Entertainment, one of the big national movie chains, is selling a monthly movie pass that's analogous to the all-you-can-eat buffet. For around $18, you buy a MovieWatcher Premium Card that gives you access to a movie a day, seven days a week.

For hardcore moviegoers, it's a hedge against soaring movie prices. For AMC, it's a bulk discount to get people into the theaters more often. (More patrons mean more popcorn and soda sales.) The movie industry has suffered recently from too many theater screens and too few bodies in the seats. So anything that brings in more moviegoers should be good for theater-owners.

Amplifying the numbers is a proven way to get attention and draw business. Did you know that there was originally only one windshield wiper to a car? Later, manufacturers doubled the wipers. (And now there are three, with the rear wipers on all those SUVs.) Shortly thereafter, the first "Double Your Money Back" offer appeared.

Question: Could you bundle two or more of what you're selling? Like the movie theater folks, you won't know what happens until you try it.

Or perhaps, conversely, you should cut down on what you produce, starting perhaps with "communications." Many organizations say too much, to too many, too often. Consequently, their messages get muddled and their customers get addled with the profusion of nonstop communication:

- Journalists despise companies that send them interminable e-mail press releases. After awhile, reporters won't even open the envelopes from companies that incessantly barrage them.

So smart companies limit their releases to only critical messages that the press actually appreciates and will use. Because these companies have reduced the number of releases, speeches, advisories, and other assorted promotional junk, they are often rewarded with more favorable treatment.

- Advertising is another communications medium that often lends itself to reduction. Increasingly, with all the new forms of targeted media now available—cable, Web, specialty trade publications, and all the rest—selective niche advertising often makes more sense than blow-'em-out mass media spending.

Are there similar strategic vehicles and products in your organization that might be subjects for reduction and therefore, targeting?

Magnifying or Minimizing the Possibilities

Let's say your team at Amalgamated TelCo has developed a new telephone service for consumers. Your job is to name your new baby. But, you're stymied.

Fortunately, you've read Chapter 3 and the wisdom of Yogi echoes in your skull: "You can observe a lot just by watchin'."

You watch the parade of names of products and services around you, and quickly observe the following: Many names are just compounds of two words that describe the brand's attributes or characteristics. These word fusions are on the newsstand: *News* + *Week* = *Newsweek*. They're at the corner: *Citibank*. They're at the tollbooth: *EZ-Pass*. They're at the gym: *Stairmaster*. They're on the cover of this book: *IdeaWise*.

Damn, they're everywhere: Earthgrains. Aquafina. Datascope. Snackwell's. Wellpoint. HealthSouth.

Your team can do that, you realize. You can *borrow* that technique and *combine* key words and turn them into new names.

Your team already has 10 terms that apply to your new phone offering. Alphabetically, they are, access, bridge, clear, connect, direct, express, flash, global, link, reach.

Now, as Ross Perot used to cackle, here's the beauty part. Your resident computer genius in the cubicle down the hall shows you a simple program for constructional linguistics. Every term joins hands with every other term.

Bingo. You're ready to magnify your possibilities:

AccessBridge	ClearBridge	DirectClear
AccessClear	ClearConnect	DirectConnect
AccessConnect	ClearDirect	DirectExpress
AccessDirect	ClearExpress	DirectFlash
AccessExpress	ClearFlash	DirectGlobal
AccessFlash	ClearGlobal	DirectLink
AccessGlobal	ClearLink	DirectReach
AccessLink	ClearReach	ExpressAccess
AccessReach	ConnectAccess	ExpressBridge
BridgeAccess	ConnectBridge	ExpressClear
BridgeClear	ConnectClear	ExpressConnect
BridgeConnect	ConnectDirect	ExpressDirect
BridgeDirect	ConnectExpress	ExpressFlash
BridgeExpress	ConnectFlash	ExpressGlobal
BridgeFlash	ConnectGlobal	ExpressLink
BridgeGlobal	ConnectLink	ExpressReach
BridgeLink	ConnectReach	FlashAccess
BridgeReach	DirectAccess	FlashBridge
ClearAccess	DirectBridge	FlashClear

FlashConnect	GlobalExpress	LinkGlobal
FlashDirect	GlobalFlash	LinkReach
FlashExpress	GlobalLink	ReachAccess
FlashGlobal	GlobalReach	ReachBridge
FlashLink	LinkAccess	ReachClear
FlashReach	LinkBridge	ReachConnect
GlobalAccess	LinkClear	ReachDirect
GlobalBridge	LinkConnect	ReachExpress
GlobalClear	LinkDirect	ReachFlash
GlobalConnect	LinkExpress	ReachGlobal
GlobalDirect	LinkFlash	ReachLink

On the other hand, sometimes it makes sense to cut down on the management or marketing possibilities. This is the general logic behind a new CEO arriving on-board and immediately wiping out layers of management. The goal is to minimize the possibilities for an organization becoming too bureaucratic, paper laden, and slothful:

- In 2001 when GE veteran Bob Nardelli moved over to run Home Depot, he didn't accept what was handed him, even though the operation was a great success.

In his first six weeks on the job, Nardelli rolled in and "over" five group vice presidents, who formed a separate management layer that his predecessors—the company's co-founders—had installed. The possibilities for inaction were reduced, and the founders were delighted.

On the marketing side, it means pruning all those product and service offerings that have multiplied ad infinitum over the years:

- That's what Procter & Gamble did with its 31 varieties of Head & Shoulders shampoo and 52 versions of Crest. Said P&G's president, "It's mind-boggling how difficult we've made it for consumers."

And so he and the organization reduced the possibilities. P&G standardized product formulas, reduced complex deals and coupons, got rid of marginal brands, axed product lines, and trimmed new product launches. It took the company a full five years to complete the bantamization of its products. But at the end of the exercise, a leaner, more profitable Procter & Gamble emerged.

Choice is a wonderful thing—but not when it throttles performance. Sometimes, reducing the possibilities is just what the organization needs to get untracked.

Choice is a wonderful thing—but not when it throttles performance. Sometimes, reducing the possibilities is just what the organization needs to get untracked.

Making It Last a Longer or Shorter Time

If only they would just keep going and going and going.

The batteries that run our cell phones and laptops have to be plugged in and recharged frequently. They're the Achilles' heel of the wireless world:

- But there's good news for workaholics. Innovations in process right now could double rechargeable battery efficiency in the next few years, and possibly quadruple it in five years, according to scientists at MIT.

At that level, you could charge your laptop overnight and leave it whirring all day.

Most battery-operated devices, from cell phones to camcorders to powerless power tools, run on lithium-ion battery technology, which appeared in 1991. Lithium is a reactive metal and especially good at storing and releasing energy quickly.

The brave new equation of batteries is this: Lighter and thinner will equal more powerful and longer lasting. Eventually, we may have lithium-polymer batteries that will be flexible enough to be laminated into any form. Further around the bend, scientists promise miniature methanol fuel cells. If you like your power exotic, then contemplate the "nanoengine" that has been built at the University of California at Berkeley. It could result in pinhead-size engines for cell phones someday.

The nanoengine is just the tip of the nanoiceberg. Nanotechnology is enveloping scientific study in the realm of the tiny. Nanotechnology measures things in nanometers, a distance one-hundred-thousandth the width of a human hair.

With nanotechnology beamed at technology, future electronic systems could be one thousand times denser and significantly cheaper, bit for bit, than they are today. The potential of such longer lasting nanotech systems in the areas of biology, technology, and elsewhere is enormous.

On the other hand, some products and services lend themselves to shorter use. From adult throwaway single-use cameras and disposable lighters to kids' individual-serve portions of macaroni and cheese to minibottles of shampoo and conditioner, not to mention the scotch and vodka that one finds in hotel rooms—limited use products are IdeaWise.

Expanding or Constricting Your Customer Relationship

It is five to six times harder to gain a new customer than it is to retain an existing one.

Therefore, your best prospect is an existing customer, whether you're selling plumbing services or tax planning. Some call it cross-selling. Some call it asset-aggregation. We just call it expanding the customer relationship—your best path to a longer and more profitable relationship.

But expanding relationships doesn't just happen. It requires an analysis of what you do that the customer needs and isn't yet buying. Clients must be introduced and encouraged to expand their relationship with you. And it's up to you to do the encouraging.

On the other hand, since 20 percent of your clients likely account for 80 percent of your profits, similarly focused efforts at constricting customers (oooh, that hurts!) is also a necessity for every organization. Essentially this means limiting services, ending enhancements, and raising prices to the 80 percent who account for 20 percent of the profits. This may not be as pleasant as increasing the services, expanding the perks, and reducing the prices for your preferred customers, but it is just as necessary.

The other side of constricting customer relationships has to do with "aiming lower." Sometimes, it's the clients at the other end of the food chain—those often overlooked by most organizations—who may be untapped gold waiting to be mined:

- The check cashing industry is one of the great unknown money-making financial institutions in our society.

Check cashers, with offices in inner cities where banks fear to tread, cash the checks of people who lack bank accounts. Check cashers deduct a healthy part of the check as a fee, and their clients get the rest of the cash. In dealing with the lower part of the financial services market, check cashers have expanded their offerings to include electronic bill paying, lending, and a host of additional—and profitable—services.

- Retailers, too, have begun to dip their toes in the waters of the less affluent. The Yamada Group, an unconventional department store and supermarket chain in Brazil, offers its credit card to poor Brazilians, who toil in the Amazon's vast off-the-books economy.

Yamada cards are good only in Yamada stores, which is just dandy with the fishermen, coconut vendors, gold miners, and street hawkers who compose the customer base.

And the business is equally fine with Yamada, which reports lower-than-normal delinquency rates and higher-than-normal profitability. According to the chain's managing director, Yamada's poor clients are so appreciative of their credit cards, they pay promptly.

- Similarly, San Francisco-based United Commercial Bank knows it can't compete with behemoth neighbors Wells Fargo and Bank of America. So it concentrates on customers the other two won't touch—new Chinese immigrants, 75 percent of whom have no credit history.

Like Yamada, UCB's default rate on loans to its specialized client base is one-tenth that of the national average. And once an immigrant finds his footing and begins to earn increased income, he is a UCB customer for life. To UCB's CEO Tomas Wu, focusing on untested immigrants is a no-brainer. When he moved to the United States from Hong Kong a decade ago, he couldn't get credit either.

Lowering the customer bar in such cases makes great business sense. So, too, might expanding or constricting the client base in your organization.

Lowering the customer bar in such cases makes great business sense. So, too, might expanding or constricting the client base in your organization.

Giving It More—or Less—Sensory Sensation

In this day of constant stimuli—with a cell phone in every driver's ear, scented soap in every bather's tub, and Tabasco in every hearty American's diet—the greater the sensory sensation, the better.

In the 1960s, the hippie cry was, "Feed your head."

Today, it's more like "Feed your senses": olfactory, occipital, tactile, taste. And the question for any marketer or manager is, How can we add to the sensory sensation of what we offer?

- Spicy chicken is an example of the new "hot thing" today—hot food. Popeyes Chicken serves up Cajun-style fried chicken that is big on zesty taste. "We're out to save America from bland chicken," say their TV commercials.

  Popeyes' $12 million ad budget is puny compared with that of its giant competitor, the Colonel. But the "bigger taste" feature is a strong point of difference, enough to drive them past Church's Chicken and past Chick-Fil-A into the second sales slot in chicken restaurants, behind KFC.

  Americans' taste buds are ready for more oomph: Mexican food, Thai food, Caribbean food.

- And what about all those aromatic products, from cosmetics to cleansers, coffees to colognes? Innovation in consumer products today more often than not involves not new products, but new flavors and scents added to existing products.

- As to touch, marketers were making products "squeezably soft" way before Charmin toilet tissue. The guy who invented the Nerf ball and all those other desktop, stress-relieving tchotchkes (look it up) have made millions.

- As to augmenting that old auditory sense, have you ever sidled up to a teenager with the top down, listening to rap or rock or hip hop? It's loud, man, loud. Rappin' loud, the theory goes, suggests an edgier, more threatening presentation. Which, in the world of rap and hip hop, is "all good." So be loud and be proud, mah man.

Question: Is there some part of your product line, or your business, where you could add more "heat" or turn up the volume? Consider emphasizing in some way what you already do.

On the other hand, turning down the sensory sensation is a bit trickier. But certainly not impossible. Taking out flavor, for example, yields a more bitter product. And sometimes, bitter is better. Bitter lemons, oranges, and grapefruits are all popular flavor-less flavors for drinks, hard candies, and pies:

- Orangina is not your mother's orange drink. It's tart, tangy, and tougher tasting than other more sissified orange nectars.

- And while M&Ms may melt in your mouth, Warheads make your mouth absolutely cringe. The hard candies, in cherry, watermelon, and other varieties, have remained the bitter choice of teenagers for many years.

Question: *Is there some part of your product line, or your business, where you could add more "heat" or turn up the volume?*

In terms of toning down the auditory sense, there is the rebirth of what we used to call "mood music." In the old days, that might have meant Sinatra, Bennett, and Como. Today, it more likely means monasterylike chanting, choral music, and Yanni.

Adding to or subtracting from the sensory sensations attached to your product or service is perhaps the most sophisticated use of magnifying or minimizing. But it may be well worth considering as a source of IdeaWise innovation.

Brobdingnagian or Lilliputian

Making things larger has become a standard course toward positive change for products and services.

"Super size that order," is music to Ronald McDonald's ears.

Making things smaller can prove equally constructive.

"Give me a one-page memo," is what Procter & Gamble tells its managers to deliver.

Adding, amplifying, magnifying, expanding, making it louder, longer, or tastier all can lead to innovation.

So, too, can subtracting, reducing, minimizing, constricting, or making it softer, shorter, or more bitter.

The sky is the limit—or the limitless—once you're IdeaWise.

CHAPTER

8

What Else Could It Be?

Arm & Hammer transformed humdrum baking soda into a refrigerator deodorant, an underarm deodorant, and a toothpaste ingredient.

When sawmills turn trees into wood planks, they also turn out piles of sawdust as a by-product. Someone had the bright idea of compressing all that "waste" sawdust and turning it into firelogs.

Inspired by his first viewing of a sculpture by Michaelangelo, composer Franz Liszt transformed the visual image into his lyric work, Il Pensieroso.

You've got something, you've made something, you own something, you've witnessed something—now, what else could it be?

Maybe it could be a mega-million-dollar industry that's been built around good old sodium bicarbonate (baking soda).

And then we have waste sawdust, as noted. Hey, your own trash should be so valuable. Wood waste has become a 160-million-ton industry all by itself.

Since you wondered, we can tell you that sawdust, wood chips, wood shavings, and shredded wood are used for:

- Animal bedding and litter.
- Fuel in municipal, commercial, and utility boilers.
- Fiberboard, particle board, and wafer board.
- Landscape mulch.
- Packaging fillers.
- Pet litter.
- Potting soil.
- Road stabilization aggregates.
- Soil treatment for clay or sandy soils.
- And, as they like to say in the ad biz, "much, much more."

Transformation in Toyland

Change has been a wonderful thing for Hasbro Toys.

For 15 years, one of the most popular action figure toy series has been the ever-changeable Hasbro Transformers.

You may be behind the times in your knowledge of toyland and therefore unaware of the latest scenario involving the Transformer Beast Machines. Well, fret no more. The heroic Maximals (fresh from the Beast Wars) have traveled back to their home planet of Cybertron, only to face a new villainous threat—the evil Predacons and their army of vehicular Transformers called Vehicons.

What is it about these gizmos that intrigue kids?

Partly it's the stark contrast of good versus evil. Partly it's the wildly imaginative names and otherworldly encounters. And hey, a little violence goes a long way these days, too.

But mainly, it's the concept that kids love. Because kids get to ask, *What else could this be?* and the machines oblige and become other things. (One Transformer starts out as a beast in battle mode, then switches to hypersonic attack mode, then becomes a ground assault creature, and finally a super robot.)

What's interesting from the Wharton School perspective is that these changes were *designed in* from the get-go. This superprofitable toy line is focused on transformation as a business. Change isn't a constant for Transformer toys—it's *the* constant.

Asking *What else could it be?* is all about transformation. Think about actors and actresses and how they "become" someone else. They transform themselves. They play new roles.

Could your service or product play one of the following new roles? Or your division or company, for that matter?

1. A new use for an existing product.
2. A new focus for your business.
3. A new method of distribution.
4. A new way to look at your audience.
5. A new use for waste materials.
6. A new way to help someone.
7. A new use for a building.

A New Use for an Existing Product

Electronic toll takers have been adapted by McDonald's franchisees in southern California to work in the restaurants' drive-throughs. The famous line "Would you like fries with that?" has been replaced by "Would you like to charge this to your transponder?" (This adapted idea came during a regular brainstorming session with franchisees.)

In Orlando, Florida, at the Disney-MGM Studios, the resident imagineers have transformed the drive-in movie theater into a restaurant. The SciFi Dine-In Theatre, one of their hit attractions, seats you in open-top automobiles in a cavernous indoor setting that resembles an outdoor park, complete with B-movie trailers flickering on big screens.

A new way to use an existing product is an old way of doing business:

- George Washington Carver thought up 300 useful articles in which peanuts could be used.
- The telephone began life as—well, the telephone. Years later, dialing a seven-digit number would bring users recorded announcements for time, weather, sports, horoscopes, you name it. Each one is a huge revenue pot for the phone companies.
- Fiberglass shows up in fishing rods, acoustic insulation, fireproofing, air filters, and textiles. (In 1941 alone, 350 patents were issued for "glass wool" products.)
- Dole and Tropicana turned their juice drinks into frozen novelties.

- Helicopters became famous as tactical devices in warfare. Today, they also herd sheep in New Zealand and ferry executives to their getaway cottages.

A hotel is just a hotel, right? Wrong! It can also be a permanent address for the well-heeled, not just a temporary residence. Innkeepers from Bali to Boston have gone on a building binge, putting up private homes attached to or affiliated with their five-star hotels.

If you're a guest who yearns to be an owner, it'll cost you. A small condo at Ritz-Carlton's Boston Commons goes for $515,000, plus an annual maintenance fee of $5,600. A stand-alone, pueblo-style house at the Four Seasons in Scottsdale, Arizona, will set you back $1.5 million. (Oh, and residents pay extra for parking, housekeeping, laundry, and other amenities.)

Humankind even benefits from urban robots, which were derived from the robots developed by Jet Propulsion Laboratories to scamper across the surface of Mars.

Why do we need 40-pound urban robots with navigation computers and cameras for vision? So they can boldly go where no human being (or dog) should have to go—into a building struck by an earthquake, or into a fire or a chemical spill.

- You may have noticed two variations here. The first is, in what new way could we use this thing, *as is?* The second is, how could this thing be *modified* to fit a new use?

Scotch tape is pretty much used as is. Helicopters have been modified (smaller, faster, more luxurious) for other uses.

Either approach could work for your business. Look at what's displayed in your catalog—or look at your prototype thingamajig locked in the vault—and ponder both possibilities.

A New Focus for Your Business

Interstate Department Stores asked itself, *"What else could we be?"* You would probably recognize the company by the new name it took, *Toys "R" Us.*

Yes, indeed. This successful retailer once was struggling along in a rut with other discount department stores. It had lots of departments, and lots of discounting, but not much of a future. Then along came a new department, toys, as the company bought *Toys "R" Us* in an embryonic state, went into bankruptcy, and emerged strictly as a toy retailer.

Question: *Is there a piece of your business, or your industry, that's ready to stand on its own? Asking* What else could it be? *can be a way of refocusing your efforts.*

Refocusing their existing business produced a category giant that now operates 1,200 stores in 27 countries. Annual sales are $11 billion. Toys broke out of the department store and stood on their own.

In much the same way, the oil-change business broke out of gas stations and car dealerships to stand on its own. This is a classic example of segmentation as a new way to focus. The convenience of 10-minute oil changes has turned Jiffy Lube and their brethren into an industry with 14,000 freestanding outlets in the United States. Not bad for a business that didn't even exist 30 years ago.

Question: Is there a piece of your business, or your industry, that's ready to stand on its own? Asking *What else could it be?* can be a way of refocusing your efforts.

A New Method of Distribution

- Our grandmothers bought their hosiery in department stores, where genteel ladies could inspect unmentionables in relative privacy. Then, Hanes found a new way to distribute—in grocery stores, of all places. L'eggs, their new pantyhose product, was delivered and stocked in much the same way that real eggs were stocked. This classic shift in distribution built L'eggs into a prominent brand.

- And this shift came long before there was a thing called the Internet and a bookseller called Amazon—one heckuva new way to distribute.

- Tupperware was a party-only player for decades. But now that more and more households have two adults working outside the home, Tupperware has to party a little harder. Their storage containers are now available in Target stores.

- Similarly, Avon cosmetics is now calling on customers in department stores.

- Even the venerable Fred Rogers, creator of the kids' TV show *Mister Rogers' Neighborhood,* found a new way to distribute his gentle message. He introduced an interactive program on the PBS website and plans to create a series of children's stories for www.misterrogers.org. Hey, it's a beautiful day in the cyberhood.

There can always be another way to physically distribute whatever you're selling. Direct mail, online, kiosks in malls, kiosks in airports, door to door—think about what else it could be.

Or maybe you're in the get-the-word-out business. You're communicating as a precursor to selling. *Same point.* There are always other ways to distribute what you're saying.

There can always be another way to physically distribute whatever you're selling. Direct mail, online, kiosks in malls, kiosks in airports, door to door—think about what else it could be.

Let's say you've been invited to give a speech to the local business council. What else could that speech be? Plenty! It could be:

- A news release sent before (with a preview) and after (with excerpts).
- An uplink to your company website.
- A possible webcast.
- A reprint in booklet form used in direct mail and as a leavebehind at customer calls.

- A mailing to the entire membership list of the sponsoring organization.

- A bylined article or Op-Ed (Opposite Editorial) piece for the local gazette.

A New Way to Look at Your Audience

- Philip Morris launched Marlboro as a woman's brand of cigarette. That sounds absurd to today's generation, but it's true. As a brand for women, Marlboro went nowhere. So Philip Morris asked, *What else could it be?* The answer was, *A brand for men.* Enter the Marlboro cowboy.

- Pontiac was once a conservative family car that competed with older brands such as DeSoto, Oldsmobile, and Mercury. In the 1960s, new management shifted the audience focus from family to youth. (Hot new cars like the GTO and LeMans helped.) "Pontiac builds excitement," the ads said, and they weren't talking to Grandpa anymore. That's still true today. Go to the Pontiac website and the first words you see are "Driving Excitement."

- When the humble hot dog takes new form as a turkey dog, a chicken dog, even a salmon dog, it appeals to a more health-conscious eater.

- Hershey Foods is trying to broaden the base of the audience that slurps chocolate milk. They want to get beyond kids in school cafeterias. Hershey has its sweet tooth set on health-conscious adults who are tired of sodas and fancy waters. Chocolate milk for baby boomers? You bet. Hershey has rolled out nationally with a fat-free chocolate milk. (So you can taste nostalgia without caloric guilt.)

• Competitor Nesquik has started packaging chocolate milk in single-serve plastic bottles, geared to adults shopping in grocery and convenience stores.

Here's a number that might surprise you: Amtrak now gets 43 percent of its total revenues from *non*passenger business. Amtrak realized several years ago that passengers alone will never make it profitable, so it went in search of new audiences such as telecommunications firms (which share wires that run along some tracks) and shippers who need express delivery of everything from dry freight to fruit.

Subsidizing passenger train service with other operations is not a new idea. It's an old idea, adapted for a new century. The Postal Service once was a major customer for passenger trains, sorting mail on board for delivery to post offices strategically built next to stations. Ironically, the decline in American rail service (which prompted the government to create Amtrak) was caused in part by the Postal Service turning to airplanes and automobiles to move the mail.

Questions: *Are you 100 percent comfortable with your core audience? Will it take you where you want to go? Maybe it's time to take a fresh look.*

Amtrak continues to carry small amounts of periodicals and first-class mail. But it carries big volumes of freight such as lemons and oranges from California, and apples from Washington State, to the East Coast.

Amtrak is under a congressional mandate to operate without federal subsidies by its 2003 fiscal year. Looking at its audience in a new way is one way to get there.

Questions: Are you 100 percent comfortable with your core audience? Will it take you where you want to go? Maybe it's time to take a fresh look.

A New Use for Waste Materials

- Once their oil and natural gas wells in the Gulf of Mexico peter out, energy companies are faced with a larger-than-life problem: What to do with the hulking carcasses of the enormous drilling platforms left behind?

Tearing down these skyscraper-tall platforms and hauling them to shore can cost more than they're worth as scrap. Some ambitious ideas have surfaced: Turn them into marine resorts for intrepid vacationers. Or, transform their isolated locations into maritime prisons.

The leading alternative for all this metal waste is a lot simpler: Convert the rigs into artificial reefs, which actually help the environment. With a little underwater cutting and rearranging, the platforms attract coral and colorful sponges to their frames. Shrimp and crab follow, and fish aren't far behind, all congregating around the old metal rigs for shelter and a bite to eat.

"It's like a McDonald's for fish," said the artificial reef coordinator for the state of Texas.

Even little scraps can be valuable—and we're not talking about the stuff you add to Fido's dinner:

- Not so long ago, two kids (ages 11 and 12) created a $100 million toy out of a scrap in pizza boxes. No, not the crust of the pizza, but the little plastic thingie that holds up the top of the box and keeps it from sticking to the hot cheese. Flip-Itz is the name for these two-inch plastic spiders that jump like tiddlywinks. (Just think of how many potential Flip-Itzes you've tossed out with the trash!)

A New Way to Help Someone

Cash is always nice. But it doesn't have to be cash to help a good cause:

- An actor asked his Hollywood friends for donations to a movie-memorabilia auction for his favorite cause: UNICEF's program to prevent HIV transmission to African newborns by infected mothers. Julia Roberts gave her wedding dress from *Runaway Bride,* and Meryl Streep her dress from *The Bridges of Madison County.* Mel Gibson donated his sword from *Braveheart,* Sylvester Stallone his boxing gloves from *Rocky.*

If you were trying to raise money for your good cause, would you even bother asking a famous person? For that matter, does your library or charity or foundation even have such a list?

Two South Florida hospitals shipped their used ventilators to South America to help children and newborns there.

Plantation General Hospital and Miami Children's Hospital sent 20 ventilators (original cost: $430,000) to several hospitals throughout Bolivia. The Florida hospitals had planned to trade in the equipment, but decided instead on a humanitarian mission. (And reaped a rightful burst of positive publicity.)

Folks in Coatesville, Pennsylvania, turned an old boarded-up hospital into a thriving resource that's restoring dignity to needy citizens in their community. The refurbished facility includes a shelter for the homeless, apartments for low-income elderly, a community health clinic, and an education center. Brandywine Hospital supports the health center with funding, staff, and volunteers. Proceeds from the hospital's thrift shop pay for overhead and some operations.

What about your company's shuttered facilities, old equipment, unused supplies? They could be helping someone, somewhere.

What about your company's shuttered facilities, old equipment, unused supplies? They could be helping someone, somewhere.

A New Use for a Building

As you've just seen, an old hospital building could be turned into a shelter and clinic. But that's by no means the only potential use for an unwanted structure.

What else could it be?

- Starbucks turns old banks and gas stations into coffee shops, keeping the facade in place and thus fitting into the character of the town.

- Train cars and entire train stations have been made into restaurants.

- Hotels and resorts have become religious retreats.

- Schools have been turned into offices and residential condos.

- Churches have become night clubs and offices. Two famous examples: The Limelight in New York City; and Arlo Guthrie's offices in a former church in the Berkshires, where scenes from the movie *Alice's Restaurant* were once filmed.

- Warehouses have been refashioned into food courts, dance halls, and lofts for residential use.

- One of Costco's no-frills warehouses in California is located in an old airplane hangar built by Howard Hughes.

- Former military bases are used as locations for shooting movies, as manufacturing sites, even for a Hilton Hotel (in Austin, Texas).

If you're looking for a site for your new business, look beyond the standard commercial real estate offerings. If you control a facility that's about to be decommissioned, ask your colleagues, *What else could it be?*

"Some painters transform the sun into a yellow spot," wrote Pablo Picasso. "Others transform a yellow spot into the sun."

Your brush is waiting.

CHAPTER 9

What Could You Eliminate?

Joe Torre had a problem: Chuck Knoblauch.

Or, more specifically, Chuck Knoblauch's arm.

Knoblauch, highly paid second baseman for the 2000 world champion New York Yankees, suddenly forgot how to throw to first base. Now such a lapse may not sound earth shattering to most of us, but for a second baseman, inability to complete the short toss to first base is positively job threatening.

Knoblauch's arm was erratic at best, uncontrollable at worst. And Torre, the all-knowing Yankee manager, was worried.

So the errant tosser was quietly sent to fielding coaches and therapists and psychiatrists and motivators of every stripe (perhaps even our old friend Tony Robbins got into the act). But nothing worked.

Knoblauch's throws just got progressively worse, until the kindly fans in Boston's Fenway Park, always willing to empathize with opponents from New York, began wearing catcher's masks to Yankee games in the event a misguided Knoblauch missile soared into the stands.

But Joe Torre is not a future Hall of Fame manager for nothing. And in the end, he figured out how to take care of Knobby's "mental blauch."

He simply eliminated the problem. He shifted his second baseman to left field, where Chuck would no longer have to make the throw to first. The result: Knoblauch became a most competent—and contented—left fielder, and the Yankees rolled.

"Eliminating," the dictionary says, "is the act of casting out or getting rid of, of setting aside as unimportant."

Being IdeaWise means getting rid of a restrictive, counterproductive, or inhibiting variable.

Being IdeaWise means getting rid of a restrictive, counterproductive, or inhibiting variable. This maneuver can be all the organization needs to introduce innovations in product, process, or performance.

Adding through Subtracting

Intuitively, when you eliminate something, you diminish it and make it less. But in business, eliminating something may, in fact, enhance the final result.

Consider these historical examples of addition through subtraction:

- Removing the tube from the tire, aka the invention of the tubeless tire, virtually eliminated punctures and sudden blowouts.

- Immortal string bean purveyor C. N. Keeney noticed that string beans were hard to prepare and unpleasant to eat if not stripped of their coarse strings. He also noticed that a few odd beans at his canning plant were stringless. Over time, he saved these aberrations, replanted them, and successfully built a harvest of stringless beans.

So the fact is that eliminating often adds value. Just ask the parishioners of Union Baptist Church in Trenton, New Jersey. A small bar a block away was a frequent source of trouble in their neighborhood. They eliminated the problem by purchasing the property (but not the liquor license). The church plans to turn the site into a youth services center.

In considering new ideas, ask a series of elimination questions:

- What can be left out of this?
- How can this be streamlined?

- What if this were divided?
- Who is affected if we split this up?
- If we took this out, what would be left?
- How would this function if we reduced it in length, size, duration, or complexity?

Such questions assess the viability of "eliminating for innovation" in organizational areas.

---

1. Eliminate process.
2. Eliminate bureaucracy.
3. Eliminate sales impediments.
4. Eliminate whole businesses or departments.
5. Eliminate unnecessary product enhancements.
6. Eliminate clients.

Eliminate clients? Yup. Even eliminating clients—particularly ones who cost you more than they're worth—can be the innovation that sparks the business.

Eliminating Process

"What processes can we eliminate?"

It is true that every business must have processes for standardization, record keeping, and control. But it is equally true that most everybody hates process.

And it is irrefutable that the more unnecessary process an organization can eliminate, the more efficient it will be. It also is irrefutable that *every* organization, department, division, unit, function, and individual can eliminate process. Beginning with paper:

- FedEx, one of the more innovative of companies, used to send clients a quarterly statement with a bonus savings amount calculated and a certificate good for the bonus amount. A customer who wanted to use the bonus had to fill in the back of the certificate, mail it to FedEx, and then wait for the next statement to deduct the amount.

Good customer benefit. But complicated and paper-a-plenty. So FedEx fixed the process by calculating the bonus and deducting it automatically from the next client invoice. Automatic credit added. Unnecessary paper eliminated. Mission accomplished.

- Attorneys at Willkie Farr & Gallagher had a paper problem, too. The prominent New York law firm represented debtors in complex bankruptcy cases involving hundred of creditors and thousands of pages of documents. Retrieving files from the firm's record room was time consuming and occasionally harrowing. Clerks often had to hop cabs or grab subways to get down to the courthouse with needed documents by trial time.

So Willkie Farr, in concert with the U.S. Bankruptcy Court in Manhattan, piloted an electronic case filing system, making entire case files available on the Internet. Although the system is not foolproof, it eliminates paper, improves efficiency, and saves subway wear and tear on the clerks.

Nonpaper processes, too, should constantly be evaluated to see what might be streamlined, expedited, or eliminated.

Take the annual meeting. (Please!) Has there ever been a more boring, anachronistic, and tedious process? (Answer: nope.) The SEC requires that every public company, every year, meet in convocation with its shareholders to discuss corporate developments. And every annual meeting is the same. You've been there. You know how it works:

> The chairman gavels the meeting to order. The corporate secretary announces that sufficient shareholders have checked in to proceed. The first corporate resolution is read aloud and discussion considered on the resolution. The vote is called for. The process is replicated for each resolution. Then the CEO delivers a formal speech. Then he or she calls for questions from the audience. Then, after the judges of election compile the votes, shareholder questions are interrupted so that the secretary can read the results of the voting and declare by how many votes, each resolution has passed. (They all pass.) Then the CEO calls for more questions. Finally, the CEO calls for adjournment, and two corporate shills—one to move, the other to second—comply with the CEO's request.

The process is interminable and an utter waste of time.

Why not eliminate parts of it? Eliminate the reading of individual resolutions, and direct the shareholders to the explanations in their proxy statements. Eliminate the speech and head right for the shareholder Q&A. Eliminate the interruption by the judges and complete the question period before reporting the voting results. Call for the results . . . call on your shills . . . and get out of Dodge.

A process this irrelevant deserves to be eliminated. And that's a guaranteed organizational win.

Eliminating Bureaucracy

"What bureaucracy can we eliminate?"

There's an appetizing question. Everybody—and we mean everybody—despises bureaucracy (except, of course, bureaucrats).

Every organization has layers, titles, protocol, and pomp that it can deep-six in a heartbeat. Beginning with the board of directors:

- Hospital systems, the result of the merger wave that has accompanied managed care, are primary felons in this regard.

Every organization has layers, titles, protocol, and pomp that it can deep-six in a heartbeat.

Typical was a Florida hospital system, the product of two anchor hospitals and several, smaller satellite hospitals acquired over many years. Each hospital joined the system equipped not only with its own overall board of directors, but also an auxiliary board for its foundation.

Invited to speak at a board retreat for this hospital system, we gazed with wonder on a gaggle of chairmen and vice chairmen, introducing themselves during the cocktail hour: "Chairman Burnside, this is Chairman Fantucket. Chairman

Steinmetz, this is Foundation Vice Chairman Von Shlepping. Foundation Chair Thymaster, this is . . ."

It reminded us of the captain's coin toss at a pro football game. Ridiculous. Superflous. Ludicrous.

Thankfully, sanity eventually prevailed. Board layers were hacked away, and today the system has one board of directors, with representatives from each of its hospitals.

Similarly, boards and hierarchical managements must be periodically pruned in a business environment where consolidation and merger are de rigueur in industries from financial services and airlines, to chip makers and railroads.

And while we're at it, what about eliminating bureaucratic organizational titles?

- Like bank "vice president." Have you ever come across a more redundant title? Everybody in the bank is a vice president.

That's why banks invented "senior vice presidents" and then "executive vice presidents" and then "senior executive vice presidents" and then "vice chairmen" and then "senior vice chairmen."

C'mon. Even bankers aren't that naive (just kidding, we love bankers).

Such bureaucratic title proliferation denigrates the worth of people who have worked diligently for promotion. Much better to eliminate the inflated titles and apply functional monikers (e.g., director of human resources, chief electronics engineer).

Or even have some—dare we say it?—fun as some Internet companies have done by renaming sales associates "idea agents," or marketing managers "dream catchers," or even re-ceptionists "directors of incoming attitudes."

Eliminating bureaucracy also applies to eliminating organizational stuffiness.

Look at your forms. The agreements and contracts you make customers sign and adhere to ought to be understand-able. Therefore, you must ask, "Can words or phrases or whole paragraphs be eliminated to aid comprehension?"

Answer, sight unseen from two consultants who've been around the bureaucratic block: Absolutely.

- The Insurance Information Institute was responsible for recommending improvements for the insurance industry. One such suggestion concerned modifying the standard 235-word insurance agreement, which began with this paragraph:

  In consideration of the provisions and stipulations herein or added hereto and of the premium, this Company, for the term of years from inception date At Noon (Standard Time) to expiration date At Noon (Standard Time) at location of property involved, to an amount not exceeding the amount(s) specified in the Declarations, does insure the insured name in Declarations . . .

  The proposed modification took just 23 words:

  We will provide the insurance described in this policy in return for the premium and compliance with all applicable provisions of this policy.

  Quite a difference.

And beyond corporate structure and forms, there is the matter of the organization's personality and what it can eliminate to help convey a more open and imaginative, less bureaucratic and imposing impression to its key constituents.

This is the critical area of not taking oneself too seriously. It's why some politicians get reelected and others don't, why some CEOs are revered and others reviled, and why some organizations could fill a reservoir with goodwill and others couldn't fill a thimble.

- Oil giant Atlantic Richfield built great loyalty through the publication of *The (ARCO) Spark,* an irreverent employee publication that offered a no-holds-barred approach to corporate truth. The innovative *Spark* was a model of candor, publishing everything from photos of refinery fires to staff letters critical of management.

This is the critical area of not taking oneself too seriously. It's why some politicians get reelected and others don't, why some CEOs are revered and others reviled, and why some organizations could fill a reservoir with goodwill and others couldn't fill a thimble.

When ARCO merged with BP Amoco in 1999, the legendary *Spark* was replaced with a toned-down publication. And the oil company's credibility with employees and its reputation for creativity presumably took a tumble.

All of which suggests that eliminating bureaucracy ought to be a frontline imperative for anyone wishing to instill the organization with new ideas.

Eliminating Sales Impediments

"What impediments to making the sale can we eliminate?"

You've delivered your products and services the same way for time immemorial. Sales are consistent, if not spectacular. So the question is, "How can you either boost existing sales or reach new markets through new sales?"

The answer may lie in eliminating ingredients in the process that may subtly be impeding greater sales.

For example, blood. That's right, blood:

- Many people object to receiving blood or blood products as part of their medical treatment, because of personal concerns or their religious beliefs. So Englewood Hospital in New Jersey, sensing the opportunity, developed a wide range of technologies to minimize blood loss and maximize the oxygen-carrying capabilities of the blood.

Englewood Hospital eliminated the delivery of blood to patients who fundamentally objected to the traditional practice. In less than a decade, Englewood's newly christened New Jersey Institute for the Advancement of Bloodless Medicine and Surgery became the undisputed national leader, performing 1,500 bloodless procedures, twice that of any other institution.

As a consequence, not only were labor costs reduced and blood usage cut by 20 percent, but Englewood's recognition and revenues exceeded all projections.

- More blood-non-letting on the other side of the country has increased the interest in, of all things, bullfights:

In central California, thousands of Portuguese Americans flock to rickety bullrings to witness a most unusual form of bullfighting that eliminates the killing of the bull.

Rather, the bull wears a Velcro patch on its shoulders that matches the Velcro tip on the matador's banderillas or paper-frilled darts. Rather than piercing the bull, the darts stick to the Velcro, to conclude the fight.

Legislators and animal protectionists love the bloodless bullfight, and aficionados of the sport don't seem to mind one bit. Moreover, as the bloodless sport has gained national publicity, new fight fans have thronged to the arena. And that's no bull.

Perhaps there are easily overlooked impediments in your products and services delivery cycle that, once eliminated, could enhance customer interest and improve sales.

Perhaps there are easily overlooked impediments in your products and services delivery cycle that, once eliminated, could enhance customer interest and improve sales.

Eliminating Businesses or Departments

"What whole businesses or departments can we eliminate?"

All but the rarest enterprises get fat over time. In robust times, businesses are acquired, departments are added, and functions are enlarged. Demand is high, so why not expand to meet it? When the economy slows, the inevitable pendulum swings back. And organizations look for businesses and departments to cut.

In the wake of the bursting of the high-tech bubble, few companies have been spared the specter of cutbacks, downsizings, layoffs, and even divestiture of businesses and departments. Firms from Intel to Apple, from Motorola to Black & Decker, have lopped off pieces of their business to remain competitive.

The best companies treat "elimination" as a business imperative:

- "Neutron" Jack Welch, legendary CEO of General Electric made his reputation as the world's foremost business manager largely through eliminating people and businesses. Back in 1981, a 45-year-old pre-Neutron Welch settled into his new job as General Electric's CEO by promptly eliminating many of the company's old-line businesses and hacking away layers of bureaucracy. In his first four years, Welch cut some 100,000 jobs, and GE was off and running on a course of growth and profitability.

Ironically, 20 years later, when the world's greatest CEO was about to retire, set up a consultancy, and publish his memoirs to share his management secrets with fellow chiefs, Neutron Jack was done in by, of all things, expansion. GE's plans to acquire Honeywell International—the coup de grâce of Welch's tenure—were upended by a diffident European bureaucrat named Mario Monti, who decided his European Commission couldn't allow the GE-Honeywell merger.

While Neutron Jack slunk into retirement, no doubt his GE successor Jeffrey Immelt planned to return to the roots of GE success, by eliminating unproductive appendages, perhaps beginning with M. Monti.

The most time-honored method of elimination is through outsourcing—where organizations figure it might be cheaper and more effective to delegate the work to outsiders and save the management and staff costs within.

Innovative approaches to outsourcing can boost any business objective, from employee retention to customer profitability:

- Royal Bank of Scotland (RBS) wanted to attract and retain highly qualified people. So it commissioned a benefits consultant to custom design an RBS cafeteria-style flexible benefits plan. The new package allowed employees to select from a wide menu of benefits, including supplemental health insurance, life insurance, child care, or even discounted vouchers for groceries. The benefits management was handled by the consultant, and RBS accrued the retention benefits.

- On the products side, beverage maker Snapple outsources the mixing and bottling of new products to avoid huge investments, time lags, and risks.

- Pharmaceutical companies outsource clinical development services to firms like Quintiles, for data management and patient recruitment in an objective, high-quality, and expeditious manner.

Sometimes, the outsourcing, itself, must be eliminated to free the organization to move onward and upward:

- In the stock market runup of the late 1990s, every commercial bank worth its full-service mantle offered a selection of mutual funds. With investors reaping returns of 30 percent, no bank could afford not to be in the business. And many banks used third parties to market and manage the funds.

But when the market worm turned in 2000, and investors saw their paper profits go up in smoke (or is that "down?"), the bank mutual fund market likewise took it on the chin. As net outflows proliferated and revenues deteriorated, the smartest choice, particularly for smaller institutions not associated with a Salomon Smith Barney or an Evergreen or a Dreyfus, was to cut the mutual fund chord and eliminate further revenue deterioration.

Eliminating Unnecessary Product Enhancements

"What product enhancements can we eliminate?"

Huh?

Why would you eliminate something you've added to spruce up the product?

Why not?

Often, the embellishments, frills, and wrinkles that organizations add to make products or services "special" eventually gum up the works. So un-gum them. Pull the plug. Get rid of them.

- Consider Continental Airlines, for many years judged the premier airline for service by J.D. Power and Associates.

Continental, under the leadership of CEO Gordon Bethune, who wrote a book about it, climbed from "worst" to "first" among airlines. And while one still will occasionally experience a Continental headset that doesn't work or a flight attendant with similar characteristics, Continental continues to improve its service through innovation.

One way it does it is to eliminate unnecessary enhancements—like first class on long flights. By ripping out its first-class section and replacing it with business-class seats (what Continental labeled, "BusinessFirst"), the airline got rid of all the frequent flier awards casher-inners hogging up its first-class section and attracted significantly more corporate travelers, whose companies will pay for business class, but not first class, on long flights.

- Not to be outdone by its rival on the elimination front, Northwest Airlines removed one of two glasses that graced dinner trays in first class. Why? "Most passengers didn't use both," said the airline. Result: annual savings of $150,000.

• The best airline eliminator is legendary Southwest which, because of its eccentric founder and former CEO Herb Kelleher, eliminated everything but the bare essentials.

Kelleher's now famous unconventional story started with a decision to fly only one airplane, the Boeing 737, to reduce maintenance, training, and inventory costs. Rather than create several expensive hubs like other airlines, Southwest chose to fly point-to-point. Instead of those spiffy flight attendant uniforms, Southwest passenger aides wear sporty polo shirts and shorts. And instead of airline food—nuts. Just nuts.

Which is exactly what Herb Kelleher wasn't. Southwest is one of the most profitable airlines in the United States (and in some quarters, the only profitable airline). The company's elimination innovation has paid off big time.

Eliminating presumed product enhancements may be counterintuitive, but time and again what top management believes will help the sales process often backfires. And it's the rare, gutsy middle manager with the nerve to decry the emperor's new clothes who can sometimes save the day.

For example, the current wave to promote entrepreneurship within the ranks is often a formula for disaster. Truly innovative companies recognize that and eliminate the managerial choices:

• Smart national chains don't want their managers using creativity to "create a warm shopping experience." Not at all. They want them hiring, firing, meeting, and greeting. That's it. Nothing more.

Eliminating presumed product enhancements may be counterintuitive, but time and again what top management believes will help the sales process often backfires.

So how do they ensure that focus?

Wal-Mart and Home Depot pipe in the same background music to every store in the system. The Gap shows the same videos from sea to shining sea. The goal of these smart retailers is to save money, establish uniformity of shopping experience, and focus local management attention on what's really important by eliminating what isn't.

- Finally, there is the true bellwether of such elimination-for-profit maximization—Saturn Corporation.

The perpetual recipient of J.D. Power's Number One Sales Satisfaction Company, Saturn sells vehicles by eliminating the number one fear of every car buyer—price haggling.

Saturn's "no hassle, no haggle" philosophy is so simple, it's positively revolutionary. Prices of all cars—new and used—are posted on the car window. There is no negotiating. What you see is what you get.

And the elimination of that once time-honored inducement to haggle has turned the auto sales business on its ear.

Saturn cars are immensely popular. And the company's reputation for quality and probity, in an industry not well known for such niceties, is well deserved.

No matter what your organization does or what industry it's in, you can absolutely introduce winning innovation by eliminating a few supposed embellishments in your products and services.

Guaranteed.

Eliminating Clients

"What clients can we eliminate?"

All customers are not born equal.

The one rule that most business managers understand— even bankers—is the 80/20 principle. Simply stated, 80 percent of your sales will be driven by 20 percent of your sales force; 80 percent of your problems will emanate from 20 percent of your staff; and 80 percent of your business will come from 20 percent of your clients.

But although most managers may "get" the 80/20 rule, distressingly few "get with it" and eliminate laggard customers.

Segment client lists and prune your customers.

- Bass Hotels & Resorts, owners of such brands as Holiday Inn and Inter-Continental Hotels, has studied up so definitively on its survey respondents, it no longer bothers sending deals to those who haven't bitten in the past. The result: 50 percent cost savings in mailings and 20 percent increase in positive responses.

- Allfirst Bank in Baltimore rewards priority customers with a special website option, which the regular schleps never see, that allows them to click to a live service agent for a telephone consultation.

Eliminating customers to enhance service delivery or product profitability can be as simple or complex as you like. Here are some of the more complicated, yet worthwhile, techniques you might try:

- *Coding.* Grading customers based on how profitable their business is to you. Each coding category is treated differently by service personnel, who are made aware of the particular client's status.
- *Routing.* Based on the client's importance to the company, he or she is routed to different organization queues. At one extreme, high-level representatives personally handle prime client inquiries. At the other extreme, recorded messages are dispatched to handle nonprofitable inquirers.
- *Targeting.* Choice customers have fees waived and receive other "hidden benefits" based on the value of their business. Less valuable clients may have no idea such perks are available.

Eliminating customers to enhance service delivery or product profitability can be as simple or complex as you like.

That's the science of eliminating less welcome clients. The simpler approach is making a basic adjustment that stimulates the desirables and turns off the un:

- The local health club—let's call it Body Bodacious—had a thorny dilemma.

Its prime market was the 20-something office workers, both Spanish and English, who worked in the big buildings that surrounded it. The problem was that the Generation Xers were turned off by all the seniors who congregated at the gym for hours, strolling around the half-mile indoor track.

Body Bodacious solved the problem by installing, as one outraged octogenarian put it, "solo maquinas." The club eliminated the track and installed, in its place, rows of rowing machines, stair-climbing machines, and lat pulldown machines; in other words, *solo maquinas.*

The elderly went elsewhere, and Body Bodacious recruited a new, young, more affluent customer base.

Innovating through eliminating clients makes good sense for any organization weighed down by the customers it keeps.

CHAPTER

10

What Could You Reverse?

The president of Meineke Discount Muffler Shops had a problem.

Not a huge problem, mind you, but a vexing one nonetheless.

When Ken Walker arrived at the company's Charlotte, North Carolina, headquarters, he found that incoming local phone calls were being answered by a receptionist at the switchboard. And incoming toll-free calls, placed mainly by Meineke franchisees, were being answered by an automated voicemail system.

The franchisees complained they could never reach a live human being. (Sound familiar?) Meanwhile, most of the local calls coming through the switchboard were either personal calls for employees or sales calls from area vendors.

Simple solution: Reverse the two systems. Now, Meineke's most important customers get to speak with a real live human being, and—more to the point—feel the company is responding to their concerns. As to the local calls from loved ones and copier salespeople—well, they'll just have to deal with it.

Vice Versa

Sometimes, the solution to a business problem is right there, in front of your nose, staring back at you. But the obvious solution can be easy to overlook.

In this chapter, we explore the *vice versa* phenomenon—reversing or, in some cases, rearranging elements you already have. There's nothing to substitute, no need to combine, no reason to magnify or minimize, nothing to eliminate.

The focus of *What could you reverse?* is on the old switcheroo. Let's take it apart and try it the opposite way. Should the engine be in the front, or in the rear? Let's turn it upside down or backward, and see what we've got.

Ready to turn the tables? You could:

1. Reverse the action.
2. Reverse the delivery.
3. Reverse the fashion.
4. Rearrange the elements.
5. Reverse your policy.
6. Reverse your strategy.

Reversing the Action

- A young railroad mechanic named Walter Chrysler saved his money and bought a top-of-the-line Pierce-Arrow motor sedan. Then he took it apart, piece by piece, and put it together again, just to see how it was made. Looking at something in reverse can be an eye-opener. (The first Chrysler automobile was the sensation of that year's auto show.)

- During World War II, Henry Kaiser found a way to speed up the construction of ships. His idea was to build whole sections such as deckhouses upside down. That way, the welders could work in a more comfortable position instead of working overhead.

- Lawnmowers always had outlets to blow the grass away. Then came chutes to attach bags for collecting the clippings. And then, some bright soul turned the tables. Instead of blowing it out a trap door, he reasoned, let's keep the grass right here—capture it and use it for fertilizing or compost. Voilà, the mulching mower.

And then there's the humble vacuum cleaner.

One night in the 1870s in a London restaurant, an engineer named Hubert Cecil Booth placed his handkerchief to his mouth, leaned close to a velvet couch and breathed in. He found a film of dirt on the other side of the cloth. Up to that point, "cleaning" a room meant using coal-powered fans to blow dirt in all directions. It might have worked in the immediate vicinity, but it turned velvet couches (not to mention drapes, clothing, etc.) into dirt reservoirs.

Engineer Booth realized that blowing had to go and that its flip side—inhaling—was the answer. So he designed fans that drew air into pillowcases to catch the dust. Queen Victoria bought two for Buckingham Palace. Soon, a small industry of men with horse-drawn machines appeared on the streets, shouting "vacuum cleaner man!" to promote a service that, well, sucked. Three decades later came Hoover, Eureka, and Electrolux with their much-improved models. (Vacuum cleaner makers were high-tech companies then—the Intels of their day.)

If you manufacture or distribute something that has an "in" and an "out" position, or an up-and-down position, or a yin and a yang, take a moment to honor the memory of engineer Booth. What would happen if you reversed the action?

If you manufacture or distribute something that has an "in" and an "out" position, or an up-and-down position, or a yin and a yang, take a moment to honor the memory of engineer Booth. What would happen if you reversed the action?

Reversing the Delivery

As long as we're talking about things with motors, let's consider the power-generating industry itself. The age-old approach has been to construct vast centralized power plants, then run wires and whatnot from these plants into the factories, stores, schools, and homes that need the power.

Now, let's reverse the delivery. There's a boomlet underway in microelectric power generation. Energy companies are building and installing small turbines in factories, stores, schools, and homes. Goodbye, distribution hassles.

On a more personal level, a reversal is underway in one of the more irritating hospital processes. Nurses or other staffers typically bring drugs to the patient. (And sitting there in your nicely ventilated gown, you wonder: Is that the right dose? Is that really my medicine?)

Questions: *What about the way you deliver the goods? Could you turn things around and bring your product or service closer to the final user?*

Now there are small pumps so patients can administer some of their own drugs. This reverse-delivery eliminates the needs for some medical support staff, and gives more control to the patient.

Questions: What about the way you deliver the goods? Could you turn things around and bring your product or service closer to the final user?

Reversing the Fashion

The fashion paparazzi and the arbiters of what's in vogue have been paying lots of attention to the straps of brassieres.

Women, it seems, have never felt that peekaboo bra straps are acceptable. But now an innovation from South America (birthplace of the thong, we might add) turns a faux pas into a fashion statement. What is this marvel? Clear-strapped bras, that's what. They've been flying off the shelves at trendy boutiques since they appeared on a Victoria's Secret catalog cover.

The point is, if colored straps are a problem, then the reverse of any color must be no color!

Hollywood can reverse things too. The fashion in movies always has been to unfold the plot in a traditional, linear way. Example: Quirky gang members come together, bicker, plan heist, pull heist. Or: Girl meets boy, girl loses boy, girl gets bra with clear straps, boy returns, happy ending:

- Did you see a movie called *Memento,* a surprise hit in 2001? Its film-noir plot literally runs in reverse. The story of murder and revenge is revealed from the last frame, first.

- Did you see the spooky *The Others,* starring Nicole Kidman? It reverses the natural order of things. The movie unfolds from the standpoint of the ghosts. (It's the living who are invisible.)

- Did you see the runaway animated hit called *Shrek?* The entire movie turns fairy-tale conventions upside down. (The princess is a kick-boxer; Cinderella and Snow White get into a tussle at a wedding.)

Most corporate names proceed in a certain order. But they, too, can be reversed.

We think the practice began with General Ambrose Everett Burnside, one of the commanders of the Army of the Potomac during the Civil War. His profuse side-whiskers, growing down along the ears to the cheeks, were his distinguishing feature and launched a trend. They were called "Burnsides." Around the turn of the century, the word experienced a linguistic transposition and became "sideburns."

Many sideburns later, the holding company for Pathmark supermarkets could have given itself the prosaic name of General Supermarkets Corporation. Instead, it transposed the words to the more attention-getting Supermarkets General.

The same is true for the Corporation for Public Broadcasting, which reversed the natural order of things.

Rearranging the Elements

- The setup men aren't getting on base. The power hitters aren't powering the ball out of the infield. That's when baseball managers often juggle their lineups.
- Customers are getting lost in the aisles. They can't find the merchandise they want. Time to redo the store's floor plan.
- The desktop of your computer is a cluttered mess. It's time to pull down that "Clean Up" command.
- The living room has gotten dull. It's boring. Time to rearrange the furniture.

For many businesses, it's also time to "rearrange."

Consider the experience of shopping in the United States. "Biggest selection" has become the mantra in specialty retailing. But as suggested in Chapter 7, Americans have a love-hate relationship with bigness.

Can big be too big? That's a real issue for the superstores or "category killers," as they are lovingly referred to in the trade. And that's something $45 billion Home Depot is noodling with, despite being named "America's most admired specialty retailer" by *Fortune* magazine for the past six years. (Leaders should always have the courage to attack themselves and challenge their own strengths.)

Enormous variety is the concept that drove this superstore chain in the first place. Although variety may be the spice of life, too much spice can lead to heartburn. First, there's the problem of managing the endless selection of Stock Keeping Units (SKUs) crammed into their humongous stores. Just watch some poor salesperson at Home Depot trying to find the right item in cartons that are 25 feet overhead. The computer may say it's in stock, but finding it is another matter. Then there is the issue of alienating consumers. The die-hard bargain hunter may relish the thousands of possibilities amidst a maze of aisles. But less driven shoppers often find the same format frustrating, or even intimidating.

Growing legions of time-pressed Americans have opted for pricier quick-hit trips to strip malls or local hardware stores. Older consumers are often turned off by the prospect of parking on the fringes of a huge parking lot, and then having to lug bulky packages back to the car. Young parents with cranky kids in tow don't have the time to figure out a bewildering store layout.

What's a category killer to do? Rearranging the elements is one answer.

Some are reducing SKUs and making their interiors more approachable with wider aisles, lower shelves, and better lighting. Others are trying to create a more festive shopping experience by adding fast food and interactive displays—anything to entice people to linger longer.

Home Depot is rearranging the elements in at least two different ways, with different kinds of stores:

- One is a scaled-down test store called Villager's Hardware. (Note the name. It says local, friendly, and accessible. Nary a behemoth in sight.) One-third the size of big daddy, modeled on the independent hardware store of Ozzie and Harriet's Main Street, this Home Depot Junior aims to attract customers who aren't willing to forage in a cavernous Home Depot store for a modest fix-it job.

- The other is a minichain of interior-design showrooms called Expo Design Center. (Home Depot already has 25 in upscale places like Laguna Niguel, California, and Boynton Beach, Florida, and says it will build 200.) This concept is directed at the home-renovation customer who's been alienated by self-service and more self-service. Expo stores have a more narrow mix of decor products, as well as specialized design consultants and installation services watched over by project coordinators. Result: High levels of customer satisfaction.

Maybe the pieces in your shop have gotten a bit congested. You might want to rearrange the elements.

One of the luxuries of success is being able to step back, take the pulse of your customer, and take a hard look at your business. Maybe the pieces in your shop have gotten a bit congested. You might want to rearrange the elements.

Reversing Your Policy

Mess with tradition and you may be playing with fire. Sometimes there are real problems that people don't want solved. They like the old-fashioned way:

- Nothing is as traditional as eating unshelled peanuts at the ballpark. Not surprisingly, you're up to your ankles in shells by the seventh inning stretch. To avoid the shell mess, concessionaire Harry M. Stevens introduced preshelled peanuts in cellophane packages. Neat solution, right? Wrong. Fans were outraged. Sales fell, complaints rose. Back to walking on shells.

  Lots of companies have gone overseas to cut labor and production costs. Charles Industries, Ltd., a Midwest manufacturer of electronic components, was no exception. But as the company grew, it encountered production problems overseas for its high-tech gear—erratic quality control, higher shipping and inventory costs, inconsistent service.
  The solution? Reverse the journey and come back home.
  The privately held company closed a plant in the Philippines in favor of expanding one in Marshall, Illinois. It closed another factory in Haiti and moved those operations to Jasonville, Indiana. Then it moved an acquired company's production lines from Nogales, Mexico, to plants closer to its home base in Rolling Meadows, Illinois.

In smaller communities, you can build a factory for about $15 per square foot, compared with $90 in a big metropolitan area. Yes, labor costs are higher than overseas. But productivity is up and rates of production rejection are way down. Since coming back home, Charles Industries has grown to $120 million in revenue.

Over at your shop, you probably have a few policies etched in granite. Sure, sure, that's the way you've always done things at Zockenfluster Corporation. Well, maybe it's time to reverse your policy.

Reversing Your Strategy

"You are young, my son, and as the years go by, time will change and even reverse many of your present opinions," wrote Plato in his *Dialogues.*

Yes, the times they are a-changing. Often the times require rethinking—even reversing—business strategies.

Why so? Start with the rapid pace of new technologies, stir in a goodly helping of shifting consumer attitudes, and season with a big dollop of global competition. That recipe has sent many a stock tumbling.

Now, bring the mixture to a slow boil with an activist board of directors, and many a CEO goes down the drain. So it's no surprise that you can pick up most any business journal, and read about some company "getting back to basics":

- Sears divested its Allstate Insurance subsidiary and other financial services to get back to tools and appliances and clothes.

- Quaker Oats, General Mills, and Procter & Gamble are all focusing (again) on their core brands and businesses.

- Bristol-Myers Squibb announces it will shed its Clairol hair care business and return to its roots as a medicines-only company.

- The British firm Holland & Holland announces it is "readjusting its sights" and giving up on becoming a major fancy fashion label. Instead, it's going back to its roots as a manufacturer of customized ("bespoke") guns and classic country apparel.

- Howard Johnson Hotels & Inns embarked on a furious expansion plan, but quality plummeted and so did perceptions of the famous orange roof. The company terminated 200 hotels and rededicated itself to getting the basics right.

- Online banks believed that the Internet would revolutionize banking. Without costly branches to maintain, they expected to offer higher interest rates on savings and lower-cost loans. The reality? Battered and bruised, online banks now are embracing their conventional cousins. They have shifted strategy, partnering with old-line financial firms or even buying branches themselves.

Sometimes, even highly regarded companies stumble and have to double back:

- Consider Midwest Express Airlines, a successful regional airline that has made service and customer orientation its differentiator.

It's a tiny airline, carrying less than 1 percent of the nation's air traffic. Yet the carrier is huge in winning awards for superior service and in achieving fierce loyalty from its business travelers.

For those who haven't had the pleasure of boarding a Midwest Express flight, here are some of the reasons for its cult following: free coffee and newspapers at the gates, wide leather seats in a 2-by-2 layout; complimentary champagne, steak, and shrimp dinners; fresh-baked cookies; attentive service; and all for a basic coach fare. Their niche: Nonstop flights to business centers on both coasts from hubs in Milwaukee, Kansas City, and Omaha. The revenue generator: Midwest Express fills its seats with company customers, instead of book-way-in-advance leisure travelers.

But there was turbulence ahead when the carrier tried to establish another hub in Indianapolis. Half of the new hub's flights were to New York's miserably congested La Guardia Airport, where delays are spelled with a capital "D."

"Here we were trying to build our brand recognition, and our flights were two hours late," fumed the airline's chairman. Solution? Reverse engines, captain. Midwest Express pulled out of Indianapolis.

- Another tale of reversal comes from Denmark, home of the toymaker Lego.

In 2000, the firm suffered only its second annual loss in its 68-year-history. What went wrong? An ill-advised diversification into technology products, baby items, and "lifestyle" products such as clothing and watches.

---

*Reversing yourself takes courage.
But that courage pays off when you realize you can
redeploy those troops, reinvest those monies,
and live to fight another day. That
sounds like a winning idea in any master plan.*

Leggo those watches, decreed management. Chief executive Kjeld Kirk Kristiansen said the loss was "embarrassing and totally unsatisfactory," and that the company would refocus on its core business of traditional Lego building bricks and other games.

Reversing yourself takes courage.

But that courage pays off when you realize you can redeploy those troops, reinvest those monies, and live to fight another day. That sounds like a winning idea in any master plan.

CHAPTER

11

What Could You Bring Back?

People want things that are hard to find. Things that have romance, but a factual romance, about them.

So began the legendary Peterman Catalog, the mail order bible for $225 Windowpane Blazers and $135 Dylan Thomas turtleneck sweaters and $180 Indian Elephant Caftans—all perfect for those chilly summer nights on the Vineyard.

From its founding in 1987, J. Peterman Company merchandise evoked another time, another place—more upscale

and passionate than those mundane offerings of L.L.Bean or
J.Crew. Right up until Peterman suffered the decidedly unro-
mantic afflictions of mounting debt and cash flow problems
that led to the company's filing for Chapter 11 bankruptcy
protection in 2000.

But then the most amazing thing happened: *Seinfeld*.

The quirky sitcom's quirky leading lady, Elaine, worked for
the quirky catalog marketer and its quirky founder, John Peterman himself—played swashbucklingly by the quirky comic
actor John O'Hurley.

Now, granted, that's a lot of quirkiness. But in television,
quirk works. And O'Hurley's Peterman became a cherished figure to the millions of *Seinfeld* faithful.

And then, the second most amazing thing happened: J. Peterman Company was reinvented. In the summer of 2001,
there on CNBC sat the real John Peterman, hawking his auto-
biography, *Peterman Rides Again*, and celebrating the reintro-
duction of a revitalized J. Peterman Company, now stronger
than ever. At the founder's side sat his company's new advertising spokesman, John O'Hurley.

You may call it "art imitating life imitating art imitating
life." We call it "bringing back." Do you have
anything in your past you can revitalize?

You may call it "art imitating life imitating art imitating
life." We call it "bringing back." Do you have anything in your
past you can revitalize?

Bringing It Back

Consumer psychologist Dr. Carol Moog explains the act of resurrecting what once was this way:

> The psychological importance of heritage may derive from the power of being a participant in a continuous line that connects and bonds one to the right to be alive, to a history that one carries forward from the living past, through death and on into the next generation; the link is a link to immortality.

What the good doctor means is that people relate to that which came before. The ideas. The products. The people. The values. The culture. The heritage of that which preceded them. There is an inherent good feeling and comfort with that which we find familiar.

"Tradition, Tradition!" is what Zero Mostel's character, Tevye, cried out in *Fiddler on the Roof*, and he was right. We crave it. We revere it. We lust for it:

- From motherhood to apple pie.
- From Old Blue Eyes to Elvis the Pelvis.
- From Big Blue to Ma Bell.
- From the Fightin' Irish to Yankee pinstripes.

Tradition rules.

That's why the cutting-edge elements of society—TV, movies, Broadway, and recorded music—don't hesitate to bring back former merchandise to reach new consumers:

- *Charlie's Angels* is brought back for Spanish television; *The Hollywood Squares* is brought back for American TV; and don't forget TV Land, the oldies-all-the-time channel.

- Alfred Hitchcock's *Psycho* is reprised with good old, lovable Anthony Perkins still in the lead; and who could ever forget all those successful sequels of *The Godfather, Lethal Weapon, Beverly Hills Cop,* and the immortal *Weekend at Bernie's?*

- Broadway is shaken to its roots when Mel Brooks' celluloid cult classic, *The Producers,* is brought back to life and is an unprecedented blockbuster.

- And the hottest thing in the record industry is the art of "covering" old songs from old artists—Buckwheat Zydeco covers Mick Jagger's "Under My Thumb," UB 40 covers Sonny & Cher's "I Got You Babe," LeAnn Rimes covers Prince's "Purple Rain," and FuzzFace covers Bob Dylan's "The Mighty Quinn."

Now, you may ask, What does all this have to do with you coming up with a big idea? Plenty.

IdeaWise could mean bringing back something from your heritage, tradition, or culture that worked then and may well work again.

IdeaWise could mean bringing back something from your heritage, tradition, or culture that worked then and may well work again.

What Could You Bring Back?

Any organization—no matter how big, how old, or how powerful—can bring back something from its halcyon days to restart its engines.

Consider Microsoft.

The most powerful company in the universe, run by the richest man in the universe, had one bummer of a year in 2000. Hounded by a wolf pack of rabid state attorneys general and battered by Washington District Court Judge Thomas Penfield Jackson, the software leader barely survived being broken up.

But it did, and in the aftermath of the government's antitrust case, founder Bill Gates sought to return the company to its precrisis luster. He would do it, he believed, by introducing an ambitious Net strategy to move Microsoft's Windows operating system onto the Internet.

To help him get there, Gates spurned the normal corporate development approach of creating a team of marketers and product managers and key executives to help him design the new strategy and products. Rather, he brought back the mechanism that had propelled Microsoft to glory in its pre-antitrust days.

Gates built a close-knit inner circle of five engineer advisers to handle everything related to the new challenge. This was precisely the same approach he had used two decades earlier to attract another brain trust to help create Microsoft.

As they say in business school, "what's good for the Gates is good for the gander." (Well, maybe they don't say that in B

School, but they should.) Microsoft's hearkening back to the good old days for inspiration is precisely what you might do to rekindle the spark in your own organization.

What might you bring back? Lots of things.

---

1. Bring back the old culture.
2. Bring back old values.
3. Bring back old messages.
4. Bring back old hits and misses.
5. Bring back old warhorses.

Any or all of these things can provide all the inspiration the organization needs to get revitalized.

Bringing Back the Old Culture

"What elements of the old culture can you bring back?"

Just as every organization has its own people, process, and products, so, too, does it have its own traditions, heritage, and unique culture.

For better or worse, no two organizations have the same culture and tradition. They are driven by different standards of performance, guided by different levels of formality, overseen by different types of people. And culture takes years to develop.

So the Tiffany style or Southwest Airlines friendliness or Morgan Stanley prestige doesn't just happen. It must be nurtured and nourished over time and then sustained for future generations to embrace.

Holding onto a culture through new management and business cycles is no easy matter. That's why there are so many "culture consultants" lurking about. Many organizations "forget what brought them to the party" in the first place.

So the Tiffany style or Southwest Airlines friendliness or Morgan Stanley prestige doesn't just happen. It must be nurtured and nourished over time and then sustained for future generations to embrace.

And often, if you can bring back that winning culture, you can win once again.

- Coca-Cola, the world's most famous beverage this side of Stolichnaya, nearly learned this the hard way.

In one of the most oft-cited marketing miscues in history, Coke's legendary former chief, Roberto Goizueta, was ready to dump the old Coca-Cola formula in favor of a sweeter "New Coke."

For about a minute and a half.

Which is about as much time as it took for Coke drinkers to storm the barricades, demanding that the revered Old Coke formula be reinstituted, no matter how controversial the taste.

Goizueta wasn't a legend for nothing. He immediately saw the error of his ways (wrongly sacrificing tradition for taste) and brought back "the real thing."

Today, New Coke is but an ancient memory, and the late Mr. Goizueta is still celebrated as a marketing genius.

- The history of The Chase Manhattan Bank is the history of the Rockefeller family and the values for which it stands—quality, wealth, charity.

For years, the Rockefeller family dominated the bank, both in management and ownership. Rockefeller relative through marriage, Winthrop Aldrich, was an early Chase CEO. His nephew, David Rockefeller, left his mark on the institution as an executive for four decades, retiring in 1980 after serving as CEO for 12 years.

Through its many mergers over the years—absorbing megainstitutions such as Manufacturers Hanover, Chemical Bank, and J.P. Morgan—today's Chase is a vastly different institution than the one that David Rockefeller led three decades ago.

Yet subsequent Chase CEOs have recognized that the Rockefeller aura is a cultural trait worth retaining. Ergo, Chase has built its private bank for wealthy clients, maintains a world-class art collection, and invites the most powerful business leaders in the world to join its International Advisory Committee. One member still in good standing on the Committee: David Rockefeller himself.

- In the 1980s and early 1990s, Continental Airlines had lost its way. The company had gone bankrupt twice, ripped through 10 presidents in 10 years, and was, as also noted, a miserable airline.

So when he stepped in as CEO in 1994, Gordon Bethune had a brainstorm to save the airline—bring back the past. The "old culture" of Continental—beginning in 1937 and continuing right up until deregulation, hostile takeovers, and multimergers clouded its mission—focused on delivering "the basics."

The most basic requirement on the list was restoring excellent service to customers. And CEO Bethune recreated the kind of culture that earned the old Continental high service marks from those who flew it.

Today, Continental is as highly rated as any airline in the world. Bethune has brought back the Continental culture.

Bringing back the tradition needn't be as seismic as turning around an airline. It can be as simple as the town of Bell Buckle, Tennessee (population 460), which each year hosts the RC & Moon Pie festival, celebrating the classic southern cola and cookie combo.

And, not coincidentally, attracting considerable recognition for both traditional products.

Bringing Back Old Values

"What values from the past can you bring back?"

Just as organizations sometimes lose sight of their heritage, they need occasionally to be reminded of their "core values"— the qualities for which they stand.

"Service," for example.

Oh sure, everyone pays lip service to client service, but few embrace the value.

- One exception was Commerce Bancorp, a "tiny" $9 billion bank in Cherry Hill, New Jersey. Despite Commerce's size,

Wall Street loved the bank for its steady growth rate, even in tough times.

Just as organizations sometimes lose sight of their heritage, they need occasionally to be reminded of their "core values"—the qualities for which they stand.

In a day of Internet banking, increased automation, and decreasing branches, Commerce took a different tack. It adopted one old-fashioned, core value to differentiate itself— customer service.

Commerce exhibited its value through such innovations as extra-long lobby hours, no-fee checking, personal small business bankers, and Sunday openings. The Commerce mantra: "If the customer wants it, we do it." As Commerce CEO Vernon W. Hill put it, "We provide all the convenience and service factors the main banks have neglected and destroyed."

And which "bank" did Commerce model itself after? Answer, according to the CEO, "Wal-Mart."

A similar value that every organization claims to possess but few have is "quality."

We used to know a CEO who said his $100 billion company stood for three things: "quality products, quality service, and quality customers." The man was a gasbag of the highest order, and didn't have a clue as to what his company stood for.

The fact is that "quality" must mean something tangible. If you really want to bring back this value, you've got to look deep into what the organization really offers.

And what about the value of "bargain pricing"? This, too, is making a big-time comeback.

- Kmart, in the midst of a renaissance with new more spiffy merchandise and the addition of some big names, like Martha Stewart, has returned to days of yore in the pricing area.

And what has it reintroduced?
Da da da da . . . Blue Light Specials.

Today, just as they were a decade ago, Kmart shoppers are caught breathless in midpurchase as the blue light starts flashing and another unadervertised promotion becomes available for less than 30 minutes.

The adrenaline rush upon hearing the loudspeaker call-to-arms, "Attention Kmart shoppers," is exciting and beautiful to behold.

Especially to Kmart CEO Charles C. Conaway, who acknowledges that bringing back the Blue Light Special has resurrected "huge brand recognition."

Beyond resurrecting the values that lead to higher sales, there are inherent values that lead to more cohesive organizations. For example, the value of "candor."

We know many CEOs who, for some reason, fear being completely candid with those who work for them. Their presumed thinking is that if they tell the employees what's really going on, they'll protest or even mutiny.

This is wrongheaded. Survey after survey indicates that employees crave knowing "how the company is doing, where it's going, and how I fit in."

What this means, as William B. Given wrote in the *Harvard Business Review* in the summer of 1946, is:

> The head of the business must expose himself to the organization as frequently as possible, both in the offices of the managers and out in the plants. . . . Wherever the executive goes, he should stimulate frank discussion.

***Survey after survey indicates that employees
crave knowing "how the company is doing,
where it's going, and how I fit in."***

Fifty-six years later, the best CEOs are still the ones who bring back candor and honesty to the employee and public dialogue.

• Lucent's Henry Schacht is an excellent example.

"Lucent!" you scream. "That disaster has cost me half of my 401(k)."

We know. We know. The company's cratering has cost us money, too. But, Schacht, on being brought back to run the company he had started, has also brought back the element of candor.

Whereas his misguided successor/predecessor sugarcoated the statements to the public and employees, returning CEO Schacht was brutally frank with his employees about the company's lost direction, immense challenges, and necessity to cut staff.

Schacht was equally candid and available with the press. And although his company's story may be a distressing one and its future remains in doubt, CEO Schacht at least deserves credit for his candor. It has helped keep the ship afloat as it navigates the storm.

Finally, what about the value of "wholesomeness"?

The so-called family values that politicians claim to revere are, indeed, worth revering. Old-fashioned concepts like respect and courtesy and fun not only remain in vogue, most people yearn to return to them.

- Minor league baseball is one place they can be found.

Most evenings during the months of July and August, most residents in the old mill town of Lowell, Massachusetts, can be found at the local Spinners' games.

The Lowell Spinners, the A League franchise of the Boston Red Sox, offer their patrons the good old value of summer entertainment that is eminently convenient and affordable.

Padded sumo wrestlers battle it out after one of the innings. Kiddie fans race around the bases between other innings. Real-life performers, dressed as "Shark McGwire" and "Clammy Sosa," march through the stands during the game. And, oh yes, on the field, the Spinners also play baseball.

Says Spinners' owner Drew Weber of the minor league phenomenon that is sweeping the United States, "There is no better, more affordable, or enjoyable family experience around."

And if you're still not convinced bringing back family values is worth something, consider this: Rush Limbaugh, that conservative gabmaster of family values rhetoric, renewed his radio contract for $250 million over nine years.

Without question, bringing back the values that people and organizations hold dear is another powerful IdeaWise source.

Bringing Back Old Messages

"What messages or slogans or logos or campaigns can we bring back from the past?"

- "Things go better with Coke."
- "Brylcreem, a little dab will do ya."
- "You'll wonder where the yellow went when you brush your teeth with Pepsodent."
- "Use Ajax (boom, boom), the foaming cleanser."

These are the memorable messages that transcend marketing history. As society gets more complex and the airwaves get more cluttered, marketers in increasing numbers are bringing back old ideas and old messages.

Why? They work, not only on a nostalgic level, but on a contemporary one.

Psychologists who study such things suggest that looking back to "heritage messages" is virtually risk-free. It suggests history and endurance and gives a sense that the product has roots, foundation, substance. Most of all, it triggers a bond between the consumer and the company.

There are many ways to bring back heritage messages.

- Personalities who made the brand famous in the first place are one such likely venue.

As proof, consider the rash of product personalities returning to public prominence after lengthy absences: Charlie the Tuna from Star-Kist; Mr. Peanut from Planters; the Jolly Green Giant from canned and frozen vegetable fame. Consumers favor the familiar.

Psychologists who study such things suggest that looking back to "heritage messages" is virtually risk-free. It suggests history and endurance and gives a sense that the product has roots, foundation, substance. Most of all, it triggers a bond between the consumer and the company.

Even Colonel Harland Sanders, who has been dead since 1980, has made a comeback as pitchman for KFC. (He's moving much more slowly, however.)

- Likewise, slogans that last are marketing gold for any organization.

Marketers yearn for a value promise that "sticks" and replace such slogans at their peril. For years, everyone knew you had "a friend at Chase Manhattan." But then the big bank got cutesy and tried to better its engrained motto. It stumbled from failed slogan to failed slogan, including one ill-advised campaign that promised, "You haven't arrived till you put the Chase behind you." Cynics suggested that once you had successfully gotten the bank "behind you" (out of your life), then you could make it.

Some firms have been smart enough to stay with a good thing:

- "We bring good things to life," says General Electric.
- "The greatest show on earth," says Barnum & Bailey.
- "It keeps going and going and going," says the Energizer Bunny.
- "They're Greeeeeeeeat!" says Kellogg's Tony the Tiger.

Bringing back the messages of products themselves is yet another way to evoke a successful bygone era.

That's what the Keds Corporation hopes to summon by renewing the relationship between kids and Keds. Even older "kids" like you, maybe.

Are there similar memorable messages in your organization's past that you can bring back for another victory lap around the marketing track?

You remember the famous navy blue footwear you used to don before mounting your banana seat bike? Well, in 2001, Keds reintroduced its original sneakers, backed up by a $7 million media campaign. The company counted on bringing back the product itself to send a message to new and old users alike that all the warmth and joy and glory of the good old days is back.

Are there similar memorable messages in your organization's past that you can bring back for another victory lap around the marketing track?

Bringing Back Old Hits and Misses

"What product hits or even misses can we bring back?"

You're sitting there, half paying attention to the TV, and all of a sudden, you're in a time capsule. A vague image begins as a small circle, set against a stark white background. As the picture sharpens, the circle becomes a flower—with seven daffodil-yellow Volkswagen Beetles as its petals.

Welcome back to the 1960s.

Retro is in: Cracker Jack. Burma-Shave. Sun-Maid raisins. Vintage baseball parks. Oldies rock and roll concerts. All evoke the emotions of a more passionate but simpler era.

Everything old is new again. So what product hits has your organization had that you might bring back?

Vehicle companies, from car companies to boat makers to scooter purveyors, are moving forward by looking in the rearview mirror.

- Designers at Ford's upscale Lincoln division are bringing back classic Continental features, such as the elongated body, distinctive front grille, and trunk spare-tire carrier to return the line to the "elegance, restraint and great proportions" of yore.
- The Bombardier Company, meanwhile, is similarly retrofitting the old pontoon boat. Only this baby has a jet-powered engine and a special compartment for the kids.

- And the hippest vehicle on the road today is the good old, two-wheeled motor scooter. Not motorcycle, mind you, motor scooter—with an average fuel consumption of 60 to 120 miles per gallon. Scooter sellers from Japan's Honda and Yamaha to Italy's Vespa and Aprilla are rolling out millions of the trendy two-wheeler classics of the 1950s. Jay Leno has three of them. Sandra Bullock has one. Even the former CEO of Ford Motor Company, Jacques Nasser, has two scooters.

And while you're reviewing your organization's past product hits, you might also take a quick glimpse at some of the "misses" over the years.

One big food company we work for reviews all the product names it has registered but discarded over the years, searching for a retro diamond in the rough.

The same review of "misses" can be undertaken in everything from rejected sponsorships and affinity programs to marketing campaigns and annual report covers.

What worked, or even failed, once may now succeed if you bring it back.

Bringing Back Old Warhorses

"Who from your past can you bring back to provide needed inspiration?"

Who says, "You can never go home again?"

In today's big stakes, high-pressure business environment, sometimes what an organization needs most is to bring back old stalwarts associated with the glory days:

- CNN, the cable news network that Ted Turner created as the great new TV force, stumbled badly in 1999.

Emblematic of the network's problems was the departure of its most productive and profitable *Moneyline* anchor, Lou Dobbs. Dobbs quit "to pursue personal business opportunities," which is business shorthand for, "He hated those to whom he reported."

Dobbs's departure opened the way for CNN's arch business rival, CNBC, to dominate in the lucrative *Moneyline* time slot. After two years of slippage, CNN finally got the message. In the spring of 2001, they brought back Lou Dobbs, more powerful than ever, to restore the network's faded glory.

- Likewise, when Honeywell International was rebuffed in its bid to merge with GE in the summer of 2001, analysts wondered whether the venerable manufacturer could remain independent.

For a year, Honeywell had lost ground and momentum, while it sat around waiting for the approval of the GE deal. CEO Michael Bonsignore bet his future on the merger, and when it ultimately capsized, it was time for him to go.

Bonsignore's replacement? The man he had replaced, Lawrence Bossidy, 66-year-old firebrand, who, as CEO of Allied Signal, originally bought Honeywell and turned it into a powerhouse. The reason Bossidy was brought back? To find "lightning in a Honeywell bottle" once again.

While these are examples of bringing back old warhorses at the highest level, your organization might have many familiar faces—retirees, alumni, spokespersons—whom you could bring back for a specific purpose.

Why, the people of the United States have even brought back another George Bush to preside at the White House. Who knows, perhaps one day they'll bring back another Clinton.

Let It Out and Bring It Back

The final proof that bringing it back constitutes an alluring business concept is the return of Crazy Eddie.

That's right, the same "Crazy" Eddie Antar, who 30 years ago built a consumer electronics retail colossus by offering name-brand products at absurdly low prices. Eddie, alas, ran afoul of the law, merely for defrauding his shareholders of $150 million.

He subsequently led federal authorities on a two-year man-hunt through Canada, Europe, Brazil, and the Cayman Islands, before being arrested in Israel.

In the summer of 2001, after a decade in the slammer, Eddie Antar was hired as director of marketing and strategic relations (but not chief financial officer) by a newly incorporated Crazy Eddie's Internet consumer electronics retailer.

So if you still don't think bringing back what worked once is a sound concept, then you, with all respect, are "Insaaaaaaane."

12

Generate First, Judge Later

Kobe Bryant takes one dribble and fires from 35 feet away. Yes!

The inbounds pass is lazy, and Kobe steals. One hop step to the bucket and he throws down a thunder dunk.

Next time down the court, with two seven-footers in his face, Kobe lofts a rainbow jumper. Swish.

Kobe Bryant is "in the zone."

There's a zone in business, too—for coming up with new ideas—that you want to land in. You want to create, to be an innovator, to sparkle with fresh thinking, to conceive ideas with genius.

This chapter is about being savvy in coming up with great new ideas. It's about the *process* of working with existing ideas, making them your own, and bringing them to life.

191

We explore three major process steps. Master them, and they will make you IdeaWise.

---

1. How to work most effectively by yourself on new ideas.
2. How to work most effectively on new ideas in a group setting.
3. And ultimately, how to begin evaluating your ideas.

Flying Solo

Let's say you're working on a problem by yourself. It might be your own business. Or, you might be functioning as a lone wolf in a corporate setting.

Earlier, we wrote about how raw ideas come your way:

1. By accident or serendipity. (The key is collecting them in some retrievable way.)

2. By systematically seeking out new information and answers that others have pioneered.

To turn those raw ideas into inspirations, you'll want to mull them over and let them tumble around in your brain.

What are the best ways to do that? The answers are as varied as climbing on a Stairmaster or sitting quietly while you listen to Mozart.

The best advice is to recognize what's worked for you in the past, and then to reinforce that successful behavior. Think back to the last fresh idea that came your way. What were you doing when you got IdeaWise? No doubt you were in a positive mental framework. (Most people are when they're solving problems.) You were probably doing something *else* while your brain was juxtaposing thoughts and funneling concepts together.

The inventor of Velcro was walking in the woods when he observed that certain seeds had grappling hooks. (The fancy name for this approach is biomimicry—studying nature's models and then imitating them.)

Here are some of the other things people were doing when they saw the light:

- Sitting in a favorite office chair, fooling around with something on the desk. (Science fiction writer Ray Bradbury said he worked best in a room full of space shuttle models and space toys; all he had to do was pick one up to trigger a fresh notion.)
- Walking through a museum or a junkyard. (Multiple stimulation could be the key.)
- Taking a shower or walking the dog. (Pleasurable but rote behavior turns on the mental burners for some people.)
- Fishing or hiking. (Favorite activities are the trick for some.)
- Jogging or working out. (Endorphins do it for others.)
- Sitting quietly, reflecting. (Many people mention a cat on the lap or classical music on the CD player as their companion.)

You know what environment is best for you.
It's your problem. It's your brain. Go to it.

Working with a Group

The term *to brainstorm* was first used in the 1920s, to describe a method of shared problem solving in which all members of a group spontaneously contribute insights and ideas. Since the practice first appeared, it's become as commonplace in many companies as a mission statement on the wall or a coffee machine in the lounge.

No, brainstorming is not a magic potion. The practice is far from perfect. A bad brainstorming session is a frivolous waste of time, a drag on morale, and a bloody bore.

An honest brainstorming session requires planning, preparation, and concentration. It can be fun and productive. It can build esprit. It can showcase surprising talents. We've led work teams and groups of people from all walks of life through hundreds of these sessions, and we've only gotten a few of those "bloody bore" evaluations. (But what do our wives know, anyway?)

An honest brainstorming session requires planning, preparation, and concentration. It can be fun and productive. It can build esprit. It can showcase surprising talents.

The beauty is, you can organize these sessions yourself, without bringing in a high-priced consultant. But before you shanghai a bunch of your colleagues into a session devoted to creating a revolutionary new lug nut, there are some rules of the road that are worth following. Here are a dozen pointers that work for us.

Effective Brainstorming

1. *Invite people who want to be there.* There's a lot of PC attention to building diverse teams—not just by race and gender but by people with different strengths (verbal, visual, mathematical, musical). All well and good. But the most important selection criterion is to invite people who are enthusiastic about the assignment and genuinely want to be in the room.

2. *Build a comfy environment.* 3M has an "Innovation & Learning Center" with sofas, books, and videos. Try to create an environment that will help your team—softer lighting, comfortable chairs, plenty of munchies.

3. *Make it fun.* There's lots of evidence that happy people are more productive people. Start the session by listening to five minutes of a Chris Rock tape. Hand out balsa wood gliders for everyone to assemble. Pass around Dilbert cartoons. Reward the first 20 contributions with a golden dollar coin.

4. *Keep it under a dozen.* More people than that, and things can get chaotic. Fewer than eight, and your output will suffer.

5. *Aim for daylight.* Most people (not all, but most) are geared to be productive during normal daylight

business hours. Schedule a brainstorming session for 7:30 P.M. and you may be greeted by droopy eyes and curled lips.

6. *Set a time limit.* Ninety minutes is ideal, two hours is tops. Anything longer, and you're spinning your wheels. (If someone suggests an all-day session, just say no.) If you decide you want more ideas, schedule another 90-minute plunge for a later date.

7. *Set some parameters.* An artist has to decide on the size of the canvas before starting to apply oils. So clearly define the problem you're trying to solve and why you've convened this merry band of ideators.

8. *Keep it upbeat.* Are you the team leader or facilitator? An optimistic, yes-we-can attitude goes a long way.

9. *Move and touch.* Many people think better with something in their hands to manipulate, or while they're moving around. Be sure to have samples, prototypes, sketches, or renderings available.

10. *Encourage piggybacking and ricocheting.* Ideas build on each other. One offbeat idea can trigger more practical ideas, like the colors in a kaleidoscope tumbling into new patterns.

11. *Record everything.* And keep all the ideas visible. Big flipcharts work as well as anything.

12. *Generate first, judge later.* The goal of a brainstorming session should be quantity, not quality. You're going to judge later. So tell everyone to park their preconceptions and their criticisms at the door.

Judgment Day

What's the world's favorite indoor sport?

No, not that one.

Okay, maybe this is the world's *second* favorite indoor sport. We're talking about the rabid human passion for criticizing, judging, and evaluating.

Way back in the Introduction, we gave you the six-step model for classic problem solving. And we devoted this book to Step 3:

---

1. Define the problem.
2. Analyze potential causes.
3. **Identify possible solutions.**
4. Select the best solutions.
5. Develop an action plan.
6. Implement and evaluate the results.

And up to this point, that's exactly what we've done.

By now, you probably have in hand a cluster of tentative new ideas. And you're ready for the next step in the process— how to select the pick of the litter and then turn your idea into something productive.

The ultimate test of any new idea is the marketplace: Does your idea solve a problem? Does it persuade customers? Does it save money? Does it make money?

Or to borrow a line from the ad agency Benton & Bowles: "It's not creative unless it sells."

But long before you take your idea to market, you can start to sift and sort your ideation output. You can evaluate.

The ultimate test of any new idea is the marketplace: Does your idea solve a problem? Does it persuade customers? Does it save money? Does it make money?

Four Initial Questions

For openers, you should answer four deceptively simple questions. A candid response to each will take you a long way down the path toward a successful new idea:

> 1. Is the idea a solution to a real problem?
> 2. Is it simple enough?
> 3. Is it timely?
> 4. Is it feasible?

Anytime you're cooking up a new product, it must solve a real problem, not an imaginary one. Dow Chemical introduced Dowtherm 209, a next-generation antifreeze coolant that was billed as "doing no harm if it leaked into the crankcase." And by the way, it cost twice as much as old-generation coolants.

The trouble was that conventional coolants hardly ever leaked into the engine. Why pay twice as much to solve a nonexistent problem? Most people didn't.

Or, consider the Susan B. Anthony one-dollar coin introduced by the United States Mint. It was simple enough to produce and the government would save $50 million a year in printing and handling costs.

But was it a solution to a real problem? Not to the public, who saw no real benefits. The coin looked like a quarter and it was ugly to boot. Sayonara, Suzy.

It's So Obvious

In hindsight, most good ideas are commonsensical. Someone suggests a new idea or a new strategy, and you wonder, "Why didn't we think of that sooner? It's so obvious?"

As you've just seen, a little common sense is a great ally when you apply any of the IdeaWise techniques:

- *Avoid wishful thinking.* Like the folks at Dow Chemical, we all want things to go a certain way. Just because you've combined *A* with *B* . . . or substituted *C* for *D* . . . or eliminated *X* from *Y* . . . or made it bigger or made it smaller . . . don't assume the world will beat a path to your portal.

- *Respect the obvious.* A dollar coin that's easily confused with a quarter—how logical an idea is that? Common sense is wisdom shared by all. It's something that registers as an obvious truth to a community. It's worth respecting.

- *Just because you can, don't automatically do it.* Not that long ago, someone at PepsiCo introduced a clear cola, christened Crystal Pepsi. How clever of someone to have engineered a way to remove the amber color from cola. But just because you've bent a few molecules, don't bend your ego out of proportion. Good judgment is based on reality, not ego. Colas are brown, not clear, and no one wanted to swallow this substitution. (Crystal Pepsi fizzled fast.)

When you ignore common sense and become illogical, your innovations have a much harder time.

- The over-the-edge but successful World Wrestling Federation combined forces with the comparatively conservative National Broadcasting Company to introduce a brand-new, smash mouth pro football league. WWF honcho Vince McMahon bragged that the XFL would "go down in television history."

It did indeed in March 2001, receiving the lowest rating ever for any prime-time network show. The XFL innovation was ill conceived, ill planned, and illogical. Nobody wanted to see stinky football. The debacle cost NBC $25 million.

- Of all the foolish dot-com ideas, none was more illogical in retrospect than online delivery services.

The online delivery model was based on a premise that it would prove more economical to dispatch dozens of messengers to hundreds of homes with thousands of bags of groceries and tubs of ice cream than it would to make all those consumers come to one store.
Huhh?

Not unexpectedly, with logic as hindsight, and after burning through hundreds of millions of dollars and scores of unwitting investors, the fraternity of online deliverers—among them, Webvan Group, Kozmo.com, Urbanfetch.com, PDQuick, and Peapod Inc.—closed the lid on their computers and bid their customers, employees, and investors adieu.

Five Forms of Risk

Damon Runyon once observed, "In all human affairs, the odds are always six to five against."

That might be a bit gloomy, but there is risk in everything we do, in every business decision we make, and in every purchase our customers contemplate.

What we're talking about in this section are the risks the *customer* perceives, and whether your particular innovation will allay them.

How does your new idea stack up on the risk-meter?

Behavioral scientists acknowledge there are five forms of perceived risks in our daily lives. So here is another list and another useful barometer as you begin to evaluate a nascent idea. Does your brainstorm eliminate, or at least soothe, one or more of these risks?

1. *Monetary risk. "I could lose my shirt."*

At $19.95 for a gizmo for your desk, it's a minor risk. At $1,995 for a combination fax-copier-scanner-printer, it's a major risk.

2. *Functional risk.* *"Maybe the thing won't work. Maybe it won't do what it's supposed to do."*

Products that are too confusing and too complex seem risky. Like a combination fax-copier-scanner-printer. Remember, most people still need help to program their VCR.

3. *Physical risk.* *"This thing looks dangerous. I could get hurt."*

Microwave ovens faced that fear in their early years. Today, people are clamoring for radiation-free electric blankets and cell phones.

4. *Social risk.* *"I wonder what my friends will think if I buy this."*

Never underestimate peer pressure and the tendency to follow the herd.

5. *Psychological risk.* *"I might feel guilty or irresponsible if I do this."*

Sellers of life insurance and 401(k) plans like to play this card the other way: You'll have guilt if you don't buy!

Six Final Checkpoints

Management maestro Peter Drucker laid down several broad reminders in his teachings.

Always look outside-in, not inside-out, he advised. Look at your business from the point of view of the customer and the marketplace. And never forget that your business is defined by the want your customers satisfy when they buy a product or service.

With that sage Druckerian advice in mind, here are six final checkpoints for the ultimate evaluation of your fledgling idea:

---

1. Does it fulfill a specific need?
2. Is it really an improvement over what already exists?
3. Is it easier to use than what already exists?
4. Is it safer than what already exists?
5. Do you have a competitive point of difference?
6. How will you bring your idea to life?

Let's probe into each of those checkpoints.

1. *Does it fulfill a specific need?* In the musical *Ain't Misbehavin'*, Nell Carter sang this immortal Fats Waller line: "Find out what they like, and how they like it, and let them have it just that way!" Well, if the need is real, and buyers perceive your idea as fulfilling that need, you're halfway home:

    -   Consumers are agitating for fast-food meals that have less fat but still taste good. Impossible? Not for a chain like Subway. And not for a handful of fledgling chains that focus on healthy food served quickly at budget prices. We're not talking sprouts and tofu here. Examples: Beefless sloppy joes, 99 percent fat-free sirloin burgers with air-baked fries, rice and noodle bowls, fruit smoothies. And for dessert: Low-fat cinnamon rolls made with applesauce instead of butter. (Have it your way, at McHealthy's.)

- Consumers also complained that potato chip bags were hard to rip open, and that jagged tears sent chips spewing in all directions. (And you thought there was anguish in your life!) So snack giant Frito-Lay and their packaging technologists initiated a new bagging process that cut the amount of force required to open the bags by 70 percent.

- The folks in Beer Land must have been out of town when Pepsi bombed with its clear cola. Because they introduced clear beer. Clear beer? What precise need does clear beer address?

2. *Is it really an improvement over what already exists?* Which means being different in ways that are meaningful to the consumer—especially to the uncommitted user:

- Early in his career, Yvon Chouinard, the founder of Patagonia sportswear, created a rock-climbing spike of chrome nickel steel so strong and light that it fundamentally changed the sport. Later he created a new curved ice ax, which gave climbers a better mooring on the smooth surface of a frozen waterfall. "I was faced with difficulties on the rock and ice," he told *Forbes* (November 26, 2001). "So I took existing products and made them better, more useful."

- First there was AM radio. Then came the superior clarity of FM. Next on the scene could be XM, which is the name of one satellite radio provider. Modeled along the lines of cable TV, satellite radio promises no advertising and hundreds of CD-sound-quality channels beamed into homes and automobiles. An improvement? Yes, but like cable TV, it will cost you—maybe $9.95 per month.

- Heinz substituted green ketchup for traditional red ketchup in its new EZ Squirt. Sure, mom goes "Yeccch!" But the kids go, "Cool!" This color switcheroo works because the audience has been clearly separated from the traditional adult influence (next up, purple ketchup).

- R.J. Reynolds spent a fortune on the first smokeless cigarette. Their theory for this supposed improvement was that smokeless cigarettes would appeal to non-smokers. Unfortunately, nonsmokers don't buy cigarettes. Something like $325 million went up in smoke (or should we say nonsmoke?) with the launch of the Premier brand. The cigarettes were hard to light, did not generate any ash (which smokers love to tap and flick), and smelled bad. Some improvement.

3. *Is it easier to use than what already exists?* People resist that which is confusing and cherish that which is simple. Basically, we want to push a button and watch it work:

   - Star-Kist tuna knows we're a society that loves convenience. Plastic pouch versions of its tuna—very easy to open—quickly captured 5 percent of the $2 billion tuna market.

- After two years and 400 attempts, researchers at Oklahoma State University have developed—trumpets, please—sliced peanut butter. This may not rank up there with laser surgery, but it sure rings the easier-to-use bell. It's a 4-inch-square, 120-calorie slice of peanut butter in a cellophane wrapper. Kids can plop it onto bread like a slice of cheese. (We assume the lads in the lab are now at work on sliced jelly.)

- The Food and Drug Administration is close to approving a powdered form of insulin that diabetics can inhale. That would be far easier than daily injections, which can be painful and can build up scar tissue. (To answer an obvious question, insulin cannot be taken by mouth because it breaks down in the stomach and never reaches the bloodstream.)

4. *Is it safer than what already exists?* It's basic human nature to want to protect your loved ones and your beloved body parts. So if your idea reduces the chance of danger or injury, it's an improvement:

- Powdered insulin scores on this count as well. Inhaling the hormone is safer than plunging a needle into your flesh.

- Englewood Hospital (mentioned in Chapter 9) created safer "bloodless" surgery—less risk in the procedure itself and no risk of receiving contaminated blood via a transfusion.

- The Butler Company introduced the first antibacterial toothbrush. Its replaceable bristles are treated with a clinically proven germ killer. Bottom line: Safer for your mouth.

- To study whale behavior in deep water, zoologists trained an agile sea lion to carry a video camera while it swam alongside the whales. The sea lion substituted for a human diver. Safer? It sure is for the human.

5. *Do you have a competitive point of difference?* Any product, any service, any company can be differentiated. It's what advertising pioneer Rosser Reeves called the "unique selling proposition." If your new idea makes sense in the context of its category, and if you have the credentials to make its point of difference believable, then you can stand out in the crowd:

- Every hospital in the country is struggling to recruit nurses. One enterprising health center focused on the fact that student nurses have to take a licensing exam (as do physicians and lawyers), and set up a huge tailgate party outside the place where the nurses-to-be took their test. A band, beer, and bratwurst produced a terrific audience for recruitment materials. How cool is this hospital, said the student nurses, and that's what differentiated the institution.

- What is different about the Hyundai automobile? Once it was the butt of jokes on Leno and Letterman. But the Korean company's U.S. management knew they had a lineup of good-looking cars (the Elantra, XG300, and

Santa Fe) at reasonable prices. Their untold story, however, was the quality and reliability of their vehicles. Good ratings from the Insurance Institute for Highway Safety were followed by top customer satisfaction rankings from car consultants AutoPacific. Hyundai captured their point of difference with the industry's first and only 10-year, 100,000-mile warranty, called the Hyundai Challenge. Showrooms started filling up with customers, and sales are up sharply while the Big Three U.S. automakers are stagnant.

- What is different about Dannon bottled water? It's a brand extension of a health and wellness image into good old H_2O, but consumers aren't swallowing that jive. Apparently a reputation for fine bacteria cultures doesn't translate into positive feelings about water purity.

6. *How will you bring your idea to life?* To sell an idea up the ladder, you'll need to address the economic factors in the execution of the idea and assess the degree of difficulty for each. That includes capital investments, time cycles, specialized personnel, and marketing costs:

- Sony adapted its original Walkman concept into the Watchman TV and the Discman CD player (a practice known as managed evolution). They had the manufacturing resources, the marketing discipline, and the distribution clout to make it happen.

- It's a similar story for Gillette and its Oral-B toothbrushes, a line acquired in 1984. At that point, there was nary a soul in toothbrush R&D. Today, Gillette has a team of 150 researching manual plaque removal. It has generated a stream of new products, from a floss made with a new fiber to its top-of-the-line Advantage toothbrush, which retails for $3.49. Oral-B sales have quintupled since 1984.

- For a PLC (Poor Little Company), a localized approach is usually the right approach. Rosemary Deahl started HeartWise Express, a health-conscious quick-serve restaurant, with a single location in Chicago. Its sales of $1.3 million now rival those of nearby McDonald's, Burger King, and Wendy's.

- It usually comes down to money to make the world go round. Consider the sad story of a computer company with a real difference: PCs for harsh environments like hot restaurant kitchens. No one was making hard-as-nails computers, so John Opincar borrowed $50,000 from family and friends and founded Iron Computer. But he relied too much on a risky initial public offering on the Internet. Not much money was forthcoming, and Iron Computer went into bankruptcy with a wonderful differentiating idea.

Innovation Means Getting It Done

Sounds like hard work, right?

It is.

The idea itself may be a new thing. But true innovation is *doing* new things.

Way back in 1969, in his book *Marketing for Business Growth*,* Harvard professor Ted Levitt offered this advice:

> Many of the people with the ideas have the peculiar notion that their jobs are finished when they suggest them; that it is up to somebody else to work out the dirty details and then implement the proposals. Since business is a "get-things-done" institution, creativity without action-oriented follow-through is a barren form of behavior.

In other words, Bunkie: It's up to you to turn that idea into action.

---

*Levitt, T. (1969). *Marketing for Business Growth*. New York: McGraw-Hill.

One Final Word: Cojones

P ardon us.
Please don't be offended. (You've come too far for
that.)

But, frankly, there is no more descriptive word to depict
the, umm, "figurative equipment" necessary to convert innovative ideas into meaningful organizational action than, well
. . . cojones.

Webster defines *cojones* as—well, actually Webster doesn't
define cojones. Nor would we expect him to.

But the *Dictionary of American Slang* defines the term
thusly:

> Cojones (coh HOH nez) *noun* Courage, audacity. . . . "requir-
> ing cojones the size of award-winning cabbages at the state
> fair"—*Car and Driver.* "You've got stainless steel cojones"—
> author James Lee Burke.

Converting innovative ideas into action requires the courage of one's convictions, unrelenting intestinal fortitude, and, well, stainless steel you-know-whats.

The sad truth is that most companies, nonprofits, trade associations, hospitals, universities, accounting partnerships, soccer teams, glee clubs, sewing societies—anything short of a sole proprietorship—aren't great incubators for innovation. They accept change slowly and new ideas grudgingly. Approving new ideas requires boldness. And "boldness," said Karl von Clausewitz, "becomes rarer the higher the rank."

Alas, how true.

We know one CEO of a major financial institution who won't blow his nose without checking first with the outside lawyers. That's not a strong inducement for innovation.

Indeed, if your boss lacks a true quest for competitiveness and is more concerned with "security," particularly of his own job, then getting new ideas approved is no easy task. That's why any generator of new ideas must be prepared first to face the bureaucratic naysayers blocking the path to action.

Caution: Blockheads Blocking the Path

An innovator must have the courage to want desperately to see his or her innovations activated. That means confronting or, at the very least, being aware of the several roadblocks that may lie ahead:

* NIH Syndrome: The Not Invented Here mentality is alive and well throughout bureaucratic America.

If coming up with new ideas isn't part of your particular job description, then you've got no right proposing that we change the system. At least, that's how it works at many organizations.

An innovator must have the courage to want desperately to see his or her innovations activated. That means confronting or, at the very least, being aware of the several roadblocks that may lie ahead.

In such places, new ideas are literally resented, because they weren't originated in "authorized idea generating sectors." Even worse, heaven forefend that you actually suggest "borrowing" someone else's idea for your own use. That is certainly an NIH no no.

- Bother: Face it, new ideas are a nuisance.

It's a hassle to have to research something new . . . approve an untested approach . . . risk launching something that may not work or getting sued because someone claims you "stole" the concept.

Organizations hate hassle. "Why bother?" is the question a laggard organization may ask. And too many don't.

- Politics: It isn't "what" you create, but "who" you know and "where" you rank that counts.

Every organization—big or small, public or private, university or hospital—is political. Internal politics is often the most dominant roadblock in an organization.

214 One Final Word: Cojones

If your idea has no management sponsors and you have little corporate clout, then the prospects for passage are greatly
reduced. That's why it's often important to cultivate strategic
internal support before taking a new idea public.

Since all corporate politics revolves around self-interest,
you've got to consider how your idea will benefit the doubters
and then work to build consensus. Modify the idea if you have
to, but don't buck the system—because 99 times out of 100,
you can't.

But if you can convince the right people and develop their
confidence, you've got a much better shot at overcoming the
roadblocks to action.

Enough with the negatives. Nobody wants to bum you out
at this late stage. Now that you understand the obstacles
standing between your idea and corporate action, here's what
it takes to get it done.

Passion

First, it takes passion.

Too few people in too many organizations are passionate
about anything. You be the exception.

Believe desperately about what you do and what your organization provides.

The Walt Disney Company nurtures its creative force by
preaching "passion." At the Disney Institute, reservation
agents are required to experience Disney through the eyes of
the customers. They stay in the resort for a night, dine in the
restaurant, use the spa and fitness center, and attend programs.

This ensures that employees understand the luxury of what they provide to customers and can more easily pass on their zest to serve.

Too few people in too many organizations
are passionate about anything.
You be the exception.

By the same token, the best public speakers—Zig Ziglar, Tom Peters, even our old buddy, Tony Robbins—are as good as they are because they are passionate about what they preach.

Without similar ardor for your own new idea, organizational roadblocks may prove too daunting to overcome. Passion for innovation, therefore, is a necessity.

Logic

Passion must be leavened by logic.

In the heyday of the Internet bubble, new economy and old economy companies alike sponsored their own "skunkworks department." A skunkworks was a group assigned to work on projects outside the usual rules. The skunkworks people were the company's true innovators. They had carte blanche to create as they wished.

Today, in the aftermath of burst bubble and declining economy, most firms are a lot less magnanimous in giving creative types their head. Companies want ideas that spring from logic, and idea merchants must comply. Indeed, as we've pointed out, IdeaWise innovations all begin with eminently logical approaches—borrowing, combining, substituting, and the like.

- In the spring of 2001 when Mad Cow Disease swept through the British beef market, McDonald's first communicated that its British beef was safe.

But nobody in Britain believed the American burger giant.

And so, on second thought, McDonald's resorted to the logic of elimination, and publicly withdrew all its meat products for four days. It then restocked its shelves with new, non-British beef.

End result: Sales fell just 15 percent during the four beef-free days, and when supplies were restocked, beef sales steadily increased.

Cojones

The final element one needs to ensure that his or her innovations see the light of day is, uh, courage.

The best innovators are passionate and logical, yes, but they also go against the grain. They're different. They're outside the norm. They're gutsy, risky, courageous.

The best innovators are passionate and logical, yes, but they also go against the grain. They're different. They're outside the norm. They're gutsy, risky, courageous.

"An innovator," according to the *Innovation Journal*, June 29, 2001 (which, one presumes, knows about such things), "takes risks, disagrees with the established wisdom . . . constantly asks irreverent questions . . . asks why, why not, how might we? She suggests ideas for improvement. Prepared to lead, she is confident about her ideas."

• Like Michael Dell.

Dell knew he couldn't compete with established computer companies for floor space in stores. Every company in the industry believed that customers wouldn't trust a mail-order company to provide such a high-end item.

Michael Dell disagreed, broke the rule, direct marketed, and built an $800 million company in five years.

• Or Christopher Reeve.

The paralyzed actor starred in the most hotly debated commercial in the history of the Super Bowl.

In 2000, Nuveen Investments produced a 60-second spot in which Reeve appeared to emerge from his wheelchair and walk to the stage. A stunned audience applauded loudly, as an off-camera announcer intoned, "In the future so many amazing things will happen in this world. What amazing things can you make happen?"

The ads drew an immediate backlash as creepy exploitation. But they also got results. Nuveen sales and share price rose dramatically after the Super Bowl airings.

As Nuveen prepared to launch phase II of the campaign, other marketers began to copy the Nuveen approach of introducing controversy in their own advertising.

• Or Matei-Agathon Dan.

This gentleman is Romania's Minister of Tourism, since you asked.

Romania's tourism industry was sagging when Minister Dan summoned up—as they say in Bucharest—a little "curaj" to conceive a bold new initiative to put his Eastern European nation on the worldwide tour destination map.

And thus was born a $40 million theme park to honor a legendary Romanian native son who made his mark right there in scenic Transylvania.

That's right. Dracula Land.

Plans call for a "horror theme park" to be completed by 2003 in the medieval city of Sighisoara, hometown of the fifteenth-century prince Vlad the Impaler. Vlad earned his reputation as the local "stakes-man" because of his penchant for impaling captured Turks. Which inspired novelist Bram Stoker to pen the original *Dracula.*

What say you of Minister Dan's brainstorm? Bats in his belfry? Perhaps.

But also, unquestionably, irrefutably, and in large quantity—cojones.

Fear Not

Finally, let it be said that even the best-laid plans—or those that aren't laid for that matter—sometimes don't work out.

So don't fear failure.

The best companies—from IBM to Citibank to Microsoft—understand that the only way new ideas can percolate freely is if failure is an accepted and expected cost of doing business.

The best ideas sometimes come from the biggest failures.

• Take the Edsel.

The Ford Edsel was among the greatest disasters in automotive history. It even looked like an Oldsmobile sucking on a lemon.

Ford planned the Edsel to give the company a full product line with which to compete with General Motors. The car was meticulously designed and crafted. And it failed miserably.

But when the Edsel bombed, Ford realized that something was changing in the auto market. The company noted that rather than the market segmenting primarily by income groups, it was now being divided by lifestyle.

This revelation, in the wake of the Edsel gloom, led ultimately to the Mustang, a car that reestablished the company as an industry leader.

Similarly, in your own case as self-appointed innovator, forget fear.

Forget:

• "I'm not good enough to be creative."
• "I'm afraid what others will say or think."
• "I may ruin my reputation."
• " It probably won't work."
• "It may turn out to be a mistake."
• "I may fail."

Forget 'em all.

Suggest. Propose. Substitute. Combine. Magnify. Minimize. Use it differently. Eliminate. Reverse. Bring it back.

In brief, be creative. Have fun. Go for it.

Become IdeaWise.

And as you savor your creative transformation and bask in the glow of your admiring colleagues, shout out loud and proud the clarion call of every idea champion:

"I'm going to Dracula Land!"

For you have earned it.

INDEX

ABOUT THE AUTHORS

STEVE RIVKIN, formerly executive vice president of Trout & Ries Inc., founded his own marketing consultancy in 1989. His clients include Kraft Foods, Johnson & Johnson, and Tiffany & Co. He is the co-author with Jack Trout of three books on marketing strategy: *Differentiate or Die* (Wiley), *The Power of Simplicity*, and *The New Positioning*.

FRASER SEITEL has been a communications counselor, lecturer, TV commentator, and teacher for 30 years, and is a prominent public relations author. His book, *The Practice of Public Relations*, is the world's number-one text, used at 200 colleges and universities. In 2000, *PR Week* named Seitel "one of the 100 most distinguished public relations professionals of the century."

Contact the authors at: www.IdeaWiseGuys.com